W9-BOM-718

Dedicated to my amazing daughters,
Bella and Grace.
Thank you both for making
my life so sweet.

Contents

Welcome to Smart Cookie! 6

Getting Started 8

The Great Outdoors 34

Desserts in Disguise 58

Happy Holidays 84

Celebrate Good Times 116

Child's Play 138

Cute Creatures 160

Formulas for Metric Conversion 181

Resources 182

Acknowledgments 184

Index 187

Welcome to Smart Cookie!

IF YOU LOVE TO DECORATE BAKED TREATS; are always looking for imaginative ways to celebrate holidays, special occasions, and day-to-day events; and love wowing your friends and family with your creations, this book is for you! But this isn't your average cookie cookbook. *Smart Cookie* will show you how to make creative, tasty, and downright adorable treats using all store-bought ingredients. Leave the baking to the bakeries and focus on the fun part—decorating!

Time is such a precious commodity these days, and if you're like me, you have more events that you want to create something sweet for than you have time to bake. *Smart Cookie* offers a solution to that dilemma. I've come up with all kinds of fun and easy ways to create treats that you will be proud to share. From birthdays to weddings to holidays, I've created fifty fun projects that I know you are going to love, and you will be shocked at how easy they are to make. Even if you have no decorating experience, you can do this! Get ready to play with cookies, frostings, candies, and lots of sprinkles to create incredible treats quickly and easily!

When I sit down and decorate cookies with my daughters, I'm carrying on the traditions that my mother, grandmothers, and great-grandmother started many decades ago. Some of my fondest childhood memories are of watching my great-grandma Josie make her famous cinnamon rolls, eating my grandma Joyce's Texas sheet cakes at parties, looking forward to my grandma Roberta's peanut butter balls at Christmas, my grandma Betty buying me Magic Shell to cover my bowl of ice cream, and my mom decorating sugar cookies with me. To me, the kitchen is a place to connect with the present, the past, and the future, and a place to spend quality time. Some days you might just be decorating cookies, but other days you might also be making memories.

The recipes in *Smart Cookie* are meant to be fun, easy, and enjoyable. I want you to be able to create amazing cookies that you are proud of. When I was developing the recipes for this book, I was constantly thinking, How can I make this easier? How can I save time? How can I keep this simple? We all lead busy lives, running from activity to activity. If you're like me, you wish you could create special treats for each and every event. You want to do something to celebrate a friend's engagement; you want to surprise your kids with something on the first day of school; and you even think St. Patrick's Day deserves something a little special.

My hope is that this book can help you with that. It can provide you with simple and clever ideas, made with ingredients you can pick up at your local grocery store, and recipes that you can throw together in no time. They are perfect for parties, holidays, and get-togethers, and I hope that creating them can even be a fun way for you to spend time with family or friends, decorating together.

If there is one message that I hope you take away, it's that you can customize any of the recipes in this book and do what works for you. If you prefer making your cookies and frosting from scratch, then by all means, make your own! For most of these recipes, you just want to make sure you find a cookie with a similar shape and size. When it comes to cookie flavors, use whatever suits your taste! Get creative, have fun, and do what works for you. Don't drive yourself crazy looking for that one ingredient you just can't seem to find; just substitute something similar for it. Your friends and family will be thrilled with whatever you make, so don't be afraid to put your own spin on these recipes. More than anything I want you to have fun, and I hope these cookies bring a smile to your face and those of your loved ones.

Happy decorating,
Christi

A note about measurements: Throughout this book I use imperial measurements (that is, teaspoons, tablespoons, cups, ounces, inches, etc.). For readers who prefer metric measurements, please consult the Formulas for Metric Conversion on page 181.

CHAPTER 1

Getting Started

It's time to have some fun and get creative with cookies! This chapter will provide you with some helpful information about the different types of cookies that are used throughout this book, as well as tips, techniques, and hints for working with chocolate coatings, frostings, sprinkles, and candies. Also included are cute packaging and display ideas for your cookies, as well as some fun ways to use any sweet cookie scraps.

Let's Talk Cookies........... 11

Frosting, Chocolate,
and Candy Coating......... 13

Cookie Pops................. 19

Sprinkles and Candy........ 21

Tools, Equipment,
and Techniques............. 25

Packaging and
Displaying................... 29

Sweet Scraps............... 32

Let's Talk Cookies

COOKIES! THAT'S WHAT *SMART COOKIE* IS ALL ABOUT. There is something just so comforting and happy about cookies. I love a homemade cookie, especially warm and fresh from the oven. Sometimes, however, we're short on time, we might not love to bake, or we would just rather put our efforts into decorating. That's when store-bought cookies shine.

The variety of cookies available in stores today is huge, from the old favorites that we all know and love, to new takes on the classics, to an incredible selection available in almost all grocery store bakeries. Every time I go to the store, I find a fun new kind of cookie.

Have you taken a stroll through your grocery store bakery lately? If you haven't, you might be very pleasantly surprised at the creative flavors and variety available there. Only a few years ago, store bakeries had a limited selection of cookies—usually chocolate chip, sugar, and white chocolate macadamia nut cookies. Times certainly have changed! Store bakeries are now offering new and creative cookie flavors, like red velvet, carrot cake, peanut butter fudge, snickerdoodle, s'mores, and salted caramel. Store bakeries are tuned into the trends, and you never know what amazing new cookies they have on hand.

Many people don't know that most grocery store bakeries will even custom-make cookies for you. On multiple occasions I have ordered unfrosted sugar cookies in a variety of different shapes from my local grocery store bakery. With a little advance notice, your store just may be able to make and bake your sugar cookies for you, leaving the decorating to you. These premade sugar cookies can be a time-saver during the busy holiday season. This is also a great option if you have kids in a school that only allows foods from commercial bakeries; it's the next best thing to homemade.

Seasonal Cookies

Cookie brands have responded to consumers' love of the holidays by creating a wide variety of seasonal cookie options. Oreo® has really done a fabulous job at creating different varieties of seasonal cookies. During the winter holidays, Oreo® offers varieties such as candy cane, winter, and gingerbread. One thing some people don't realize is that brands will sometimes make exclusive flavors for certain stores, so don't assume that all stores carry the same selection. Store bakeries also have a great selection of seasonal, holiday, and special event cookies, such as cookies shaped like stars and footballs—you never know what you might come across walking through the bakery. When I stumble on seasonal cookies in shapes that are hard to find the rest of the year, such as hearts, I often pick some up to store in my freezer for use at a later time.

Sandwich Cookies

What's a sandwich cookie? A sandwich cookie is any cookie with a top, a bottom, and a filling in the center. They are cookies you can gently pull apart into separate pieces and then put back together. From Oreo® cookies to Nutter Butters®, there are many brands and flavors and even gluten- and sugar-free varieties. You can find sandwich cookies in a variety of shapes, such as round, square, and rectangular, and even in fun shapes like leaves. What makes sandwich cookies special is that they are perfect for making cookie pops! Cake pops are wildly popular, but making them may be something of a challenge. Cookie pops, on the other hand, are quick and easy to make. Cookie pops are one of my go-to holiday treats. They taste delicious, they are cute as can be, and you can easily package them for gift-giving by slipping a food-safe, cellophane bag on top of the cookie and tying it closed with a festive ribbon.

Soft Cookies

Some recipes in this book call for soft cookies. Soft cookies can easily be cut with a cookie cutter or a knife, without the cookie crumbling. Some brands offer chewy versions of their cookies, and these typically work well with cookie cutters. Sugar cookies can be a bit of a wild card when it comes to softness. As a rule of thumb, a puffier sugar cookie tends to be on the softer side whereas a flatter sugar cookie usually tends to be firm.

Frosting, Chocolate, and Candy Coating

FROSTING

YOU KNOW THE SAYING "THE FROSTING ON THE CAKE"? Well, that frosting is every bit as good on a cookie! The recipes in this book all use store-bought frosting, allowing you to focus entirely on the decorative aspect of your cookie creations. If you like to make homemade frosting, by all means, whip up some buttercream from scratch!

Coloring the Frosting

I usually keep vanilla and chocolate frosting on hand and doctor them to suit my needs. With food coloring you can tint your frosting any and every color under the rainbow. I love McCormick® food colorings, especially their neon colors. To create dark, intense colors, such as a deep red or royal blue, a gel food coloring usually works best. For black frosting, I like to start with chocolate frosting and add black food coloring to achieve the desired shade.

Flavoring the Frosting

You can do more than just color your frosting—you can flavor it, too! I keep a variety of McCormick® flavor extracts on hand to flavor my frostings. Some of my favorite extracts to stir into my frosting are raspberry, peppermint, lemon, vanilla, coconut, and strawberry. I start with half a teaspoon of extract for a 16-ounce can of frosting and adjust from there. Just remember: You can always add more, but you can't take too much away.

There are other ways to flavor your frosting as well. I love to mix a tablespoon or two of caramel ice cream topping into my frosting for a caramel flavor. A tablespoon or two of smooth peanut butter mixed in with your frosting can create a fabulous peanut butter vanilla or peanut butter chocolate flavor.

If you find store-bought frostings a bit too sweet for your taste, sometimes a pinch of salt can help temper the sweetness just a bit. There are also products such as Duncan Hines® Frosting Creations™ flavor mixes made to be mixed into your frosting to transform it into flavors such as cotton candy, mocha, and orange crème. Finally, whenever a recipe in this book calls for white or vanilla frosting, feel free to use cream cheese–flavored frosting if you prefer.

Thickening the Frosting

Just as with homemade frosting, if you want to thicken your store-bought frosting you can add confectioners' sugar to it. Empty the can of frosting into a mixing bowl. Add ¼ cup confectioners' sugar to the frosting and mix well with a stand mixer or a hand mixer. You can add more confectioners' sugar, a teaspoon or two at a time, until the frosting reaches the desired consistency.

Melting the Frosting

Many of the recipes in this book use melted frosting. You can easily melt frosting by microwaving it in a microwave-safe bowl for 10 seconds. Remove it from the microwave and stir well. You want your frosting to melt to the consistency of syrup. If 10 seconds is not enough time, return it to the microwave and heat it for an additional 5 seconds, remove it, and stir. Repeat this process until the frosting reaches a syruplike consistency and you can pour it. As the frosting cools, it will thicken back up and you may need to reheat it a couple more times before you are finished decorating.

Melted frosting works wonderfully to coat cookies quickly and easily. Before the frosting dries, it is great for holding onto sprinkles and decorations, and it dries to a smooth finish. I have tried a number of different frosting brands, and Duncan Hines® Creamy Home-Style seems to melt the best and dries to a nice finish. I highly recommend sticking with this brand variety for any recipe that calls for melted frosting. Whipped-style frostings do not work well for melting, so avoid them for this purpose whenever possible.

COOKIE ICING

For many recipes in this book, I prefer to use Betty Crocker® Decorating Cookie Icing. This icing comes in an easy-to-use pouch that you simply knead and then squeeze out through the built-in tip. The icing dries to the touch quickly and after four hours becomes quite firm, somewhat like a royal icing. If you prefer to use homemade icing, whip up a royal icing recipe whenever Betty Crocker® Decorating Cookie Icing is called for.

~·~

⌒ CHOCOLATE ⌒

THERE IS NOTHING I LOVE MORE than a rich, delicious bar of high-quality dark chocolate; it's truly one of life's sweetest treats. When it comes to melting chocolate, however, that same chocolate can be a bit difficult to work with. While its taste is second to none, it requires careful tempering to achieve the desired result. Tempering is a method of carefully and precisely heating and cooling chocolate, within a strict temperature range. When you melt chocolate, the fat molecules separate. When you temper chocolate, you put those molecules back together. Tempering gives chocolate a smooth, glossy appearance; allows it to harden; and provides that snap when you bite into it.

⌒ CANDY COATING ⌒

CANDY COATINGS—WHICH COME IN CHOCOLATE, VANILLA, and other flavors, as well as a wide variety of colors—are much easier to work with than actual chocolate. Candy coating—also called melts, confectioners' coating, almond bark, summer coating, and wafers—looks and tastes like chocolate, but is much more forgiving to work with. The big difference between chocolate and candy coatings is that chocolate has a cocoa butter base, whereas candy coatings have an oil base, such as palm kernel oil. Candy coating is less expensive than chocolate, and even beginners can have great results working with it.

Chocolate brands, such as Ghirardelli®, Guittard®, and Barry Callebaut, even make candy coatings. Candy coating such as CandiQuik® comes packaged in a tray that you can use to melt it in, making for incredibly easy cleanup. Candy coatings are available in almost all grocery stores as well as craft and hobby stores.

If you're comfortable tempering chocolate, then by all means, substitute chocolate for the candy coatings that are suggested in this book. If, however, tempering chocolate seems a bit daunting, then candy coatings are a great option. Many people use chocolate chips and are not happy with the results. Chocolate chips have certain additives to help them retain their shape when baking, which can affect the tempering process. I love to use chocolate chips for decorating, but not for melting.

Working with Candy Coating

Whether you are using chocolate or candy coating, it's important not to overheat it. It's always best to heat slow and low to avoid burning chocolate. It's also very important to keep it away from water! Water can make chocolate or candy coating turn gritty and even seize, so make sure all your equipment is completely dry. You never want to use liquid food colorings to color your chocolate or candy coating. I prefer to buy my candy coating in the wide variety of colors that are available, as opposed to coloring it myself. Wilton® Candy Melts® are a great option if you're looking for a wide range of color options. If you want to color your candy coating yourself, make sure to use an oil-based food coloring.

Sometimes candy coating may be a bit thick, which makes it slightly difficult to handle. There are a few ways to thin out your candy coating to make it easier to work with. I personally like to use paramount crystals (available online and through baking supply stores), but others use vegetable oil or shortening. It's always best to start with a little—no more than a teaspoon—and stir it into your candy coating until it's melted and fully combined.

Melting Candy Coating

Almost all candy coatings come with detailed melting directions on the package. Make sure to read and follow the directions carefully. Overheating will cause your chocolate to thicken and be very difficult to work with. If you find yourself with a candy coating that does not have directions, you can melt it in your microwave or use a double boiler. To melt it in the microwave, place the candy coating in a microwave-safe bowl and melt at 50 percent power for 30 seconds. Remove from the microwave and stir very well, since the candy coating will often retain its shape, even when melted. If the candy coating is not yet melted, heat it again at 50 percent power for another 30 seconds, remove, stir, and repeat this process until the coating is melted. To melt the candy coating in a double boiler, place the candy coating in the top pan of a double boiler over hot, but not boiling, water. Allow the candy coating to melt slowly, stirring until smooth.

CANDY WRITERS

Also called candy decorating pens, candy writers are small tubes containing meltable candy coating that can be used like a pen. I love working with candy writers, especially for attaching candies and sprinkles to cookies, almost like a candy coating glue, and for getting candy coating exactly where I want it. They come in a variety of colors and have melting directions on the package. I usually heat up water in the microwave, not to the point of boiling, in a coffee mug. Then I place my pen into the hot water, carefully, with the top of the candy writer sticking out of the water (you do not want the pen fully submerged). This melts the candy coating, and you can return your candy writer to the mug of hot water between cookies, keeping it ready to use. Once done, you simply let it cool and the candy coating inside will harden and be ready for the next time. In place of a candy writer you can use candy coating, applied either with a toothpick or through a piping bag.

Cookie Pops

WHEN MAKING COOKIE POPS, prepare the candy coating according to package directions, then gently twist open the sandwich cookies. Use a lollipop stick or straw to make an indentation in the filling, creating a place for the cookie pop stick to be placed. Dip the stick or straw into the candy coating, then place it onto the cookie filling in the area where you made the indentation.

Using a spoon, place approximately 1 to 2 teaspoons of additional candy coating on top of the stick or straw that you have already put on the cookie, and then place the second part of the cookie back on top to create the sandwich. Put the cookie pops in the refrigerator to chill for at least an hour. By doing this, the candy coating in the center of the cookie sets, and helps hold the stick or straw, and cookie, together. If you don't follow this process, cookies can very easily fall off the stick when dipping them into chocolate or another coating.

By placing your cookie pops in the refrigerator to chill, you also shorten the amount of time it takes your candy coating to dry after dipping your cookie pops. This is important because hot drippy candy coating can be quite a mess, and it can be a challenge to get sprinkles and decorations to stick, since they'll tend to slide off. Even slightly chilled cookie pops will make the dipping and drying process much easier.

When I dip cookies into candy coating, I always hold the cookie above my candy coating container for a good 30 to 60 seconds, allowing excess candy coating to drip back into the bowl. Sometimes I very gently tap the cookie on the side of the bowl, especially if there appears to be a lot of excess candy coating on the cookie. Be very gentle, though, or you will tap your cookie right off its stick and right back into the candy coating. A little patience and a gentle hand work wonders when you're handling cookies and candy coating.

Sprinkles and Candy

SPRINKLES

WHILE CHOCOLATE MAKES ME HAPPY, SPRINKLES MAKE ME SMILE. I absolutely adore sprinkles; they are like little colorful containers of happiness. I love them so much that I store mine in mason jars on a shelf in my kitchen, on display to look at all the time. A handful of sprinkles is all you need to decorate cookies, cakes, cupcakes, and more. I've never been good at decorating cakes or cupcakes, and instead rely on the generous use of sprinkles as a decorating strategy. Grocery stores seem to consistently be increasing their sprinkle selection, and hobby and party supply stores often have twice as many options.

If you have a local baking supply store, chances are good that you'll find an amazing variety of sprinkles year-round. For holidays, make sure to check the holiday product displays for sprinkles: They are often stocked in those areas instead of the actual baking aisles. Sprinkles are used throughout this book, so I thought it would be a good idea to go over the basic varieties.

The most common type of sprinkles, also referred to by some as jimmies, are what you see most on cupcakes, doughnuts, and soft frosted sugar cookies. They look like little sticks or lines and even add a bit of crunch to whatever confection they're used on. They come in a variety of colors and in multicolor, but I prefer to buy containers of single-color jimmies and then mix my own color combinations. Having a container of red, a container of white, and a container of green would allow you to mix colors for Christmas, Valentine's Day, and St. Patrick's Day.

Nonpareils

Nonpareils are those teeny-tiny sprinkles that are shaped like balls. They are most often seen in white or rainbow colors. Be careful when using these: They have a tendency to go everywhere!

Quins

Fun, festive, and creatively shaped little sprinkles, quins vary from hearts to circles to stars; the variety of shapes and sizes is amazing. I love to keep heart and circle shapes in a variety of colors and sizes on hand all the time because they can be used in so many ways in decorating your cookies. Stores often offer seasonal shapes and styles during the holidays and I always try to stock up on these, especially after the holiday when they go on clearance.

Crystal Sugar

A large, coarse, decorative sugar, crystal sugar is translucent and comes in a wide variety of colors.

Sanding Sugar

Much finer than crystal sugar and almost as fine as granulated sugar, sanding sugar comes in a variety of colors, and sometimes even has a bit of a sparkle to it. When using sanding sugar, I usually place a bowl below my cookie and pour the sanding sugar directly onto the cookie, letting the sanding sugar that does not stick to the cookie land in the bowl to be reused. This gives better coverage and a more dramatic effect than sprinkling it on a little at a time.

Did you know that you can make your own colored sugar? While not quite the same as sanding sugar, which is usually a bit coarser, homemade colored sugars are just as much fun to work with. Place ½ cup of granulated sugar in a jar with a tight-fitting lid, and add a drop of liquid food coloring. Place the lid on the jar, making sure it's on tightly, and shake well until the color is combined. Due to the added moisture from the food coloring, this colored sugar can sometimes clump, and adding just a pinch (no more than ¼ teaspoon) of cornstarch to the mixture helps get rid of the clumping. Store in an airtight container.

Edible Glitter

Edible glitter doesn't even look like glitter, but rather it has a flakelike consistency and a translucent appearance. It sparkles and shines on treats, but it does not look like the glitter you pick up in the craft aisle. It adds a bit of texture and a beautiful, whimsical quality to your treats.

Dragées

These are little, hard, round balls that are most often silver, but come in other colors as well. When I was growing up, my mom used them often on sugar cookies. They are quite hard, so many people enjoy the decorative aspect of them, but they can be a challenge to eat, so I use them sparingly.

Pearls

Pearls refer to the little round candies that look like, well, pearls! These are typically not as hard as dragées, and they come in a variety of shapes and sizes. In addition to pearl sprinkles, SweetWorks® makes small candy balls called Pearls™, which are larger than the pearl sprinkles.

Sugar Decorations

Not technically a form of sprinkles, but, more often than not, you'll find them in the store right next to the sprinkles. Sugar decorations are fun shapes and decorative accents that reflect almost any theme you can think of. Sugar decoration designs range from images for baby showers to over-the-hill parties, holiday gatherings, and even your favorite characters. These are cute, edible decorations that are often made of royal icing or pressed sugar. They vary in size from itty-bitty at around 1/8 inch to extra large ones many inches in diameter; in this book we'll use sizes that are just right for decorating cookies!

CANDY

THIS BOOK IS JAM-PACKED WITH FUN WAYS to use candy for decorating. The variety of candy on store shelves can make your head spin! From old favorites and classics to dazzling new varieties, there is a candy for anything and everything. In the last few years, we have seen a trend of bringing back some nostalgic candies from years past, and candy stores are stocking their shelves full of both new and vintage options.

Holidays are a great time to stock up on seasonal candies, such as candy corn at Halloween and candy canes in December. Check the expiration dates: Most candy lasts for a year or two, allowing you to stock up on it when it's available and use it throughout the year. Holiday candies are often found in the seasonal section of grocery stores, so make sure to wander out of the candy aisle and over to the holiday products. Also watch the checkout areas for candy; not only can you find a different selection of products than in the candy aisle, but you can also purchase small, single-serving packages, which sometimes are all you need.

Most of the candies used in this book are decorative in nature, and you can switch them up and use different varieties if you like. For example, where I use a Jordan almond, feel free to use a peanut M&M®. It's all about having fun, getting creative, and enjoying what you're doing and what you're making.

CANDY EYEBALLS

And then there are candy eyeballs. I always have a supply of candy eyeballs on hand, and you will see them used throughout this book in recipes including Falling Leaves (page 45), Smart Cookie (page 157), and Good Doggie (page 168). They come in a variety of sizes and are available at most grocery stores and hobby stores, right next to the sprinkles. If you don't have candy eyeballs, you can always use a round piece of white candy and a little black frosting or coloring from an edible marker.

Tools, Equipment, and Techniques

TOOLS AND EQUIPMENT

DON'T LET THE WORD *TOOLS* SCARE YOU: There is nothing heavy-duty going on here! Having on hand some very simple tools, many of which you probably already own, will help you in decorating cookies.

Cookie cutters aren't just for cookie dough! You can cut most soft cookies—and even hard cookies like graham crackers—with cookie cutters. My most useful cookie cutters are my round, square, and heart-shaped cutters. If you don't own a set of graduated round cookie cutters, it's a great investment that can be used with cookies, candies, brownies, and biscuits.

Other items that are handy to have in your kitchen are cutting boards, which make a nice work surface; mini tongs or clean tweezers for dipping cookies in candy coating; wire racks; waxed or parchment paper; baking sheets; small spatulas; toothpicks; small knives; a mini-size rolling pin; a piping bag; and two pairs of scissors—one to cut candies and one to cut packaging. I also find it helpful to keep a few baby spoons in my tool collection: They are very useful when you need to get a scoop of frosting or candy coating in just the right spot.

EDIBLE MARKERS

Also referred to as food writers, food coloring pens, gourmet writers, and food coloring markers, edible markers are food-safe markers that are available in most grocery and hobby stores. These fun markers allow you to literally draw on your cookies!

TECHNIQUES

I HAVE TRIED TO KEEP THIS BOOK SIMPLE and fun, and not heavy in techniques or technical details. There are a few very simple techniques that are used throughout this book to get the frosting or chocolate onto the cookies.

Frost

To frost a cookie, simply spread frosting onto the cookie with a small offset spatula or even a dull knife.

Pipe

To pipe frosting onto a cookie, squeeze the frosting through a pouch, pastry bag, or even a large zipper-style freezer bag, with a small hole or decorating tip at the end. For a number of recipes in this book I use Betty Crocker® Decorating Cupcake Icing, which comes in an aerosol can and includes four different decorating tips in the lid that you can change out. This frosting is ready to pipe, straight from the can.

Dip

To dip a cookie into candy coating or frosting, you do just that—dip it! When I dip my cookies, I also use my spoon to help spoon frosting or candy coating over the cookie as well, which is the best method I've found for fully covering cookies. When dipping, make sure your container is deep enough to allow you to dip the cookie adequately, and wide enough so you can also use your spoon while dipping. I like using a 2-cup glass measuring cup for dipping; it's wide enough to fit most cookies into yet deep enough to easily dip the cookies. After dipping cookies into candy coating, I hold my cookie over the container and allow the excess frosting or candy coating to drip off. I prefer to place them on a sheet of waxed or parchment paper to dry.

Pour

Many recipes in this book use melted frosting (see page 15). To melt frosting, simply place it in a microwave-safe bowl and heat it for approximately 10 seconds, remove from the microwave, and stir well. It should be about the consistency of syrup. If it is still too thick, heat for another 5 seconds, remove, and stir again. Repeat this process until the frosting reaches the desired consistency. The frosting does firm back up as it cools, so sometimes you'll need to reheat it once or twice while you are decorating.

To pour, you can either pour the frosting directly from the bowl onto the cookie, or you can use a spoon or knife to spread the melted frosting over the cookie. Either method works; it's simply a matter of personal preference. Place the cookies on a wire rack, and place the wire rack on a baking sheet lined with waxed or parchment paper before pouring the frosting onto the cookies. This allows the excess frosting to drip through the wire rack and collect in the baking sheet.

Packaging and Displaying

PACKAGING

COOKIES ARE GREAT FOR GIFT-GIVING. You can give a plateful of cookies or a single cookie in pretty packaging. There are so many great options, with more hitting the market every day. I always keep food-safe clear cellophane bags on hand; they are perfect for packaging cookies and almost any other baked good. For a quick and simple way to dress up your cookies, place a cookie, or cookies, into a cellophane bag, secure it with some pretty ribbon, and add a gift tag. Baking supply stores, hobby stores, and online retailers offer an amazing array of colorful treat boxes, tubes, and food-safe printed gift bags that you can mix and match to fit almost any theme.

You can also repurpose items you have and fill them with cookies for gift-giving. Wide-mouth mason jars look sweet when filled with cookies, and you can even reuse those round Pringles® cylinder chip containers by cleaning them out and re-covering the outside with decorative paper or fabric.

DISPLAYING

IF YOU THINK OF YOUR COOKIES the way you think of cupcakes or cakes, you'll find there are many great ways to display them. You can display cookies on cake stands, cupcake stands, plates, and platters. You can also use baskets and pails to display cookies. If you can sit or stand a cookie on it, you can use it as a display piece! Set a plate on top of a bowl and you have a makeshift stand! Get creative and think outside the box.

Sometimes I like to take a decorative element from my cookie, such as sprinkles or a type of candy, and create a bed of them to place my cookies on. This is a fun and simple way to add color and texture to your displays. For example, try serving Goody Goody Gumballs (page 149) in a big bowl full of gumballs, or O Christmas Tree cookies (page 100) on a bed of crystal sugar akin to snow—both sure to be hits with your guests. Your cute cookie creations are not only perfect for dessert, but they can be a part of your decorations as well.

To display cookie pops, I like to use decorative pails or containers, fill them with uncooked white rice or beans, and stand my pops up in the container. Rice and beans are not the prettiest, so I top them with candies or even sprinkles. If my pops have SweetWorks® Pearls™ on them as a decorative element, I might cover the rice or beans with more of those Pearls™. I always like to pull a decorative element from the cookie into the display if I can. If you aren't sure what to use, candies like M&M's® or Skittles® always look great.

Sweet Scraps

SOME OF THE RECIPES in this book will leave you with some leftover cookies or cookie crumbs. While it is perfectly acceptable to just enjoy these cookie bits as is, there are also a number of fun ways for you to use them.

Cookie-Topped Brownies

Using your favorite brownie mix or recipe, you can sprinkle cookie crumbs on top of your brownies just before baking them. If you have enough cookie crumbs you can even stir some into your brownie batter.

Cookie Bark

You can make an incredibly easy cookie bark by stirring cookie crumbs and pieces into melted candy coating and then spreading it out on a baking sheet lined with waxed or parchment paper. Once the candy coating sets, you can break the bark into pieces. One of my favorite cookie bars uses white candy coating, Oreo® cookies, broken-up pretzel pieces, and candy corn! It sounds like a crazy combo, but it's absolutely delicious.

Cookie Shake

Blend crushed cookies with ice cream and milk in a blender to create a delicious shake with a bit of crunch. You can even rim the top of your glass by dipping it into chocolate sauce and then dipping it into cookie crumbs. Full or half cookies make a great garnish on top of your shake.

Leftover Frosting

While I don't usually find myself with leftover frosting, my favorite thing to do with it is to spread it between two graham crackers and create frosting sandwiches. My mom would do this when I was a child and store them in the refrigerator. The crunchiness of the graham crackers with the sweet creaminess of the frosting always made for a delightful treat.

Cookie Frosting

Finely crushed cookies, stirred into frosting, add a wonderful flavor. I love to make chocolate cupcakes and top them with vanilla frosting into which I have stirred crushed chocolate cookies.

Cookie Parfait

Layer cookie crumbs with ice cream, or even pudding, and add hot fudge or caramel sauce, whipped cream, and sprinkles for a tasty cookie parfait sundae.

CHAPTER 2

The Great Outdoors

Bring a little bit of nature inside with these cookies inspired by the great outdoors. From rainbows in the spring to snowmen in the winter, there is a little something for every season. These cookies are perfect for seasonal parties and outdoor celebrations, and can even be paired with cookies from the Happy Holidays chapter (page 84).

Over the Rainbow ... 37

Fun Flowers ... 39

By the Campfire ... 43

Falling Leaves ... 45

Adorable Acorns ... 48

Sweet Snowmen ... 51

Nice Nests ... 53

Down by the Seashore ... 55

Over the Rainbow

GROWING UP, I LOVED RAINBOWS *and wanted them everywhere. I even had rainbow-colored mini blinds. Thankfully, my rainbow window-covering phase was short-lived and now I appreciate them far more in their natural state. No matter what your age, there is always something magical about spotting a rainbow in the sky. These little rainbow cookies let you enjoy a rainbow whenever you like.*

Makes 12 cookies

12 Keebler® Fudge Stripes™ cookies

12 ounces blue candy coating

½ cup blue sprinkles (such as nonpareils)

6 Airheads Xtremes® Sweetly Sour Belts

120 miniature marshmallows

1. Place the Fudge Stripes™ cookies into the freezer for at least 20 minutes.

2. Prepare the blue candy coating according to package directions.

3. Line a baking sheet with waxed or parchment paper. Working one cookie at a time, take a cookie out of the freezer, dip the striped side into the candy coating, then place the cookie, chocolate-side down, on the waxed paper. Garnish with the blue sprinkles or nonpareils.

4. Repeat with the remaining cookies. Let the cookies dry for at least 20 minutes. If necessary, reheat the candy coating according to package directions, and let cool slightly. A thick, slightly cooled coating will work best.

5. Place approximately a teaspoon of the blue candy coating on opposite sides of the cookies, where the rainbow will be attached to the cookie.

SMART COOKIE TIP:

*The Airheads Xtremes®
Sweetly Sour Belts work best
if you cut them and prepare
them the day before. I cut
mine in half and then drape
them over the side of a cup,
helping create the bend in
the rainbow. The center of
the candy belt should sit
on the rim of the glass, with
both sides of the candy
hanging down—one on the
inside of the glass, one on
the outside.*

6. Working one cookie at a time, dip the two ends of an Airheads Xtremes® Sweetly Sour Belt into the candy coating, then place it on the candy coating covering the cookie. Hold the candy belt in place with one hand and immediately start placing the miniature marshmallows around it to help brace the candy belt and support it. If there is not enough candy coating on the cookie for all your marshmallows, then dip one side of the marshmallow into a bit of candy coating prior to putting the marshmallows onto the cookie. Each side of the rainbow should have five marshmallows at the rainbow base, with a total of ten marshmallows per cookie.

7. Repeat with the remaining cookies. Allow to dry for at least 2 hours.

Fun Flowers

EVEN IF YOU DON'T HAVE A GREEN THUMB, *you can make this little flower garden grow! Don't worry: If you don't have the edible adhesive, you can just use drops of candy coating or a candy writer in its place. After your cookie flowerpots have set, add green candy coating to the center of the flowerpots. Just before that candy coating sets, place a sweet little flower lollipop into the center, just like planting a flower! Finish with green sprinkles and some sugar decoration leaves.*

Makes 8 cookies

**32 Murray Sugar Free®
shortbread cookies**

**Wilton® Dab-N-Hold™
edible adhesive**

**6 ounces green
candy coating**

**Green sprinkles
(about ¼ cup)**

**16 green sugar
decoration leaves**

**8 flower-shaped candy
lollipops**

1. Starting with one cookie, apply dots of the edible adhesive to the top side of the cookie. Immediately place another cookie on top.

2. Place dots of edible adhesive on the top of the second cookie, top with a third cookie, place dots of edible adhesive on the third cookie, and place a fourth cookie on top; this will create the flowerpot.

3. Repeat with the remaining cookies, creating eight flowerpots in all. Set aside and allow to dry for at least six hours.

4. Prepare the candy coating according to package directions.

5. Place the cookie flowerpots onto a baking sheet lined with waxed or parchment paper. Using a small spoon (a baby spoon works well for this), spoon a small amount of the candy coating into each cookie flowerpot to fill the center.

SMART COOKIE TIP:

These cookies are great for spring and would also be darling for baby showers, bridal showers, and birthday parties. Depending on the color of the lollipops you use, you could even create holiday versions.

6. Dust the candy coating in the flowerpot with green sprinkles.

7. Put a dab of candy coating on the back of the sugar decoration leaves and place two on each flowerpot as though they were coming out of the center, one on each side.

8. Cut the stick on the flower-shaped candy lollipop down to the desired size, and insert the stick into the candy coating in the center of the flowerpot. Repeat with the remaining cookies. Allow to dry for at least two hours. Take care not to move the cookies until they have completely dried.

By the Campfire

THE FIRST THING THAT COMES TO MIND *when I hear the word* campfire *is roasting marshmallows. There is just something so simple and special about sitting together around a fire and roasting marshmallows. While it's not always easy to get everyone out and around a campfire, it is easy to make these cookies anytime you want.*

Makes 12 cookies

20 Life Savers® orange hard candies

20 Life Savers® red hard candies

10 Life Savers® white or yellow hard candies

12 miniature marshmallows

12 small pretzel sticks

1 (7-ounce) pouch green Betty Crocker® Decorating Cookie Icing

12 sugar cookies

36 Tootsie Roll® Chocolate Midgees

1. Preheat the oven to 350°F. Line a medium-size baking sheet with parchment paper.

2. Unwrap the Life Savers® candies and place in a large zipper-style freezer bag. Crush the candies using a rolling pin or a small mallet.

3. Spread the crushed candies out on the baking sheet lined with parchment paper. The crushed candy should be spread out, but the pieces should be touching each other.

4. Place the crushed candy in the oven for approximately 5 minutes, or until the candy has melted. Remove from the oven and allow to cool for at least 15 minutes, or until it's cool to the touch.

5. Once the candy is cool, use your hands to break the melted candy into pieces approximately ¼ to ½ inch wide and 1 to 2 inches long. Set them aside.

6. Gently place a miniature marshmallow on the end of each pretzel stick.

SMART COOKIE TIP:

The "flames" are made by melting crushed Life Savers® in your oven for just a few minutes and then letting the melted candy cool and harden. This is the only recipe in this book that requires you to turn on your oven, and it is totally worth it!

7. Prepare the icing according to package directions.

8. Working one cookie at a time, spread cookie icing on top of the cookie. Immediately place three Tootsie Roll® Chocolate Midgees onto the cookie icing, placing them in a formation similar to logs in a campfire.

9. Place three to four pieces of the melted Life Saver® candies onto the cookie, as campfire flames, using the chocolate candies to help prop them into place until the icing is dry.

10. Place a pretzel with marshmallow onto the cookie. Repeat with the remaining cookies. Allow to dry for at least four hours.

Falling Leaves

LIVING IN ARIZONA, FALL IS MY FAVORITE TIME *of year. It is the end of many long months of heat, and the beginning of a few wonderful months spent outside. Unfortunately, we don't see many of the typical fall colors, so I often take matters into my own hands and decorate and bake using reds, golds, and oranges to evoke that fall feeling. These leaf pops—an awesome autumn treat—are perfect for fall school festivals and parties.*

Makes 12 cookie pops

12 ounces candy coating in color(s) of your choice

12 leaf-shaped sandwich cookies

12 lollipop sticks or straws

½ cup sanding sugar in color(s) matching your candy coating

24 candy eyeballs

Black edible marker (optional)

1. Melt the candy coating according to package directions.

2. Gently twist apart the sandwich cookies and place them on a baking sheet lined with waxed paper.

3. Using a lollipop stick, make an indentation in the filling of each cookie. Dip the end of the lollipop stick into the candy coating, covering about 1 inch of the stick, and then gently press it into the indentation in the filling.

4. With a spoon, place approximately 1 to 2 teaspoons of the candy coating on top of the stick where it is pressed into the filling and immediately place the other half of the cookie on top of the coating. Repeat with the remaining cookies. If necessary, reheat the candy coating according to package directions.

5. Place the cookies in the refrigerator for at least 1 hour.

6. Remove the cookies from the refrigerator. Reheat the candy coating according to package directions.

SMART COOKIE TIP:

These leaf cookies would also be great for Christmas. Use green candy coating and green sanding sugar to cover the cookie, and add red candies to create holly. Trader Joe's sells maple leaf cookies year-round, as do some grocery stores.

7. Working one cookie at a time, holding onto the stick, dip the cookie into the candy coating, allowing the excess coating to drip off.

8. Sprinkle the sanding sugar over the candy coating.

9. Place the cookie onto the waxed paper–lined baking sheet and immediately place two candy eyeballs onto the cookie. Repeat with the remaining cookies. Allow the candy coating to set until firm, at least 2 hours.

10. If you'd like, you can use a black edible marker to draw smiles onto the cookies.

Adorable Acorns

THESE DARLING LITTLE ACORN COOKIES *make for fabulous treats that are perfect for fall parties. They are simple to put together and the recipe can easily be doubled or tripled, if desired. You can fill a large glass bowl or jar with these cookies for a quick table centerpiece that can turn into dessert at the end of your meal. For gift-giving, try filling a mason jar with these sweet acorn cookies and finishing it off with some ribbon or raffia.*

Makes 24 cookies

12 Nutter Butter®
cookies

12 small pretzel sticks

6 ounces chocolate
candy coating

2/3 cup chocolate
sprinkles

1. Cut the Nutter Butter® cookies in half through the center point. Break the pretzel sticks in half.

2. Melt the candy coating according to package directions.

3. Dip the cut end of a cookie into the candy coating, covering only about one quarter of the cookie. Immediately sprinkle the chocolate sprinkles over the candy coating.

4. Dip the end of a pretzel stick into the candy coating and then attach it to the candy coating on the cookie; this becomes the acorn's stem.

5. Place the cookie on waxed or parchment paper. Repeat with the remaining cookies. Allow them to dry until the candy coating is firm to the touch.

Sweet Snowmen

I HAVE TO BE HONEST: *I don't come across snowmen very often where I live in Arizona, yet something about them always seems so sweet and fun. If I can't build snowmen, at least I can build cookie snowmen! These snowmen are easy to put together, and each snowman is made up of three individual cookies, making them great for sharing.*

Makes 4 snowmen

12 large, soft round cookies

1 (16-ounce) can vanilla frosting

White crystal sugar (about ½ cup)

1 (7-ounce) pouch blue Betty Crocker® Decorating Cookie Icing

¼ cup white Tic Tac® Freshmints

28 black SweetWorks® Pearls™

4 orange candy–coated sunflower seeds

12 black SweetWorks® Sixlets®

8 small pretzel sticks

SMART COOKIE TIP:

For a fun flavor twist, stir a few drops of peppermint extract into your frosting and use chocolate cookies.

1. Using cookie cutters, cut four cookies into large circles, four cookies into medium circles, and four cookies into small circles. The small circle cookies should be at least 1 ½ inches in diameter.

2. Ice all the cookies with the vanilla frosting, leaving the top two thirds of the four small cookies unfrosted in the area that will become the hats.

3. Sprinkle the frosted areas with crystal sugar.

4. Prepare Betty Crocker® Decorating Cookie Icing according to package directions. Squeeze the icing onto the unfrosted part of the four cookies to create hats. Immediately place the Tic Tac® mints along the base of the hat, and one at the top.

5. To create four snowman faces, take the cookies that have blue hats and place on each two Pearls™ for eyes, one sunflower seed for the nose, and five black Pearls™ for the mouth.

6. On the four medium-size cookies, place three Sweet-Works® Sixlets™ down the center of the cookie as buttons.

7. Arrange the cookies on plates in shapes of snowmen, placing the small pretzel sticks next to the medium-size cookies to represent snowman arms. Note that the pretzel sticks and cookies are not stuck together, but rather arranged on the plate to look like snowmen. Allow to dry for at least two hours.

Nice Nests

THESE BIRD'S NEST COOKIES *are made using one of my family's favorite holiday treats, once made by my grandma Bonnie. These haystack cookies are no-bake, combining crunchy chow mein noodles, melted butterscotch (or peanut butter) chips, and melted chocolate candy coating. They've always reminded me of bird's nests, so I figured I'd make them into just that. By adding a few jelly beans or chocolate candy eggs, they are transformed into bird's nests.*

Makes 12 cookies

6 ounces butterscotch or peanut butter chips (about 1 cup)

6 ounces chocolate candy coating (about 1 cup)

1 (5-ounce) can of crispy chow mein noodles (about 2½ cups)

60 candy eggs or jelly beans

12 chocolate bakery-style cookies

SMART COOKIE TIP:

SMART COOKIE TIP:

I prefer to use chocolate cookies, but feel free to use other cookies, such as peanut butter. While I simply sit the bird's nests on top of my cookies, you can also frost the cookie first and then place the bird's nest on top of the frosting to affix it there, if you'd like.

1. In a large microwave-safe bowl, combine the butterscotch or peanut butter chips with the chocolate candy coating. Place the bowl in the microwave for 1 minute. Remove and stir well. If it's not fully melted, return it to the microwave at 50 percent power for another 20 to 30 seconds. Remove and stir well. If necessary, repeat for one more heating cycle.

2. Once the coating is fully melted, allow it to cool for 2 to 3 minutes, then combine the crispy chow mein noodles with the coating, stirring well to fully combine.

3. Using a large spoon, drop the noodles into twelve equal servings on a baking sheet lined with waxed paper. Once the mixture has completely cooled, use your hands to gently shape each into a nest.

4. Place approximately five candy eggs or jelly beans into the nests after shaping them. Allow the nests to dry, about 2 hours, prior to placing each on top of a large bakery-style cookie.

Down by the Seashore

I LOVE THE BEACH. *There is just something so peaceful about the ocean. Living in the desert, I don't get to see the ocean as often as I'd like, so I'm always looking for ways to bring a bit of the beach to me. These beach-themed cookies are super-quick to make. I used Betty Crocker® Decorating Cupcake Icing in both blue and white to make them. This icing comes in aerosol cans and includes different piping tips that you can change out. If you can't find them, any blue and white frostings will do.*

Makes 12 cookies

36 vanilla wafers, finely crushed

White and gold crystal sugars (about 1 tablespoon each) (optional)

1 (8.4-ounce) can Cloud White Betty Crocker® Decorating Cupcake Icing

1 (8.4-ounce) can Sky Blue Betty Crocker® Decorating Cupcake Icing

12 large, round sugar cookies

Sugar pearls (optional)

12 sugar decoration seashells and starfish

1. To create the effect of sand, combine the crushed vanilla wafers with the white and gold crystal sugars and set aside. If you don't have crystal sugars, don't worry: The wafer crumbs will work on their own, too, but the sugars give it a nice bit of sparkle.

2. Prepare the icing according to package directions, and place the desired tips on both the white and blue frosting.

3. Cover the top third of the cookies with white frosting and immediately sprinkle with a light coating of crushed vanilla wafers and crystal sugars.

4. Pipe a line of white frosting immediately below the area that is covered with crushed wafer crumbs. Use blue frosting to cover the rest of the cookie. Using an up-and-down motion while applying the frosting will help replicate the look of waves.

SMART COOKIE TIP:

For a different look, decorate these cookies with candy fish or even Goldfish® crackers. For the seashells and starfish, I used sugar decorations that I found at my local baking supply store, but any seashell-shaped or starfish-shaped candy will work. Chocolate seashells would be perfect on these as well.

5. If you're using sugar pearls, sprinkle a few onto the area covered with crushed wafer crumbs. Place a sugar decoration seashell or starfish on the cookie where desired.

CHAPTER 3

Desserts in Disguise

The only thing cuter than a cookie is
a cookie disguised as another dessert.
This chapter will show you how to easily
create delicious desserts that just might
fool your friends and family and leave
them saying, "That's a cookie?"

Lovely Little
Layer Cakes...61

We All Scream for
Ice Cream Cones...63

A Dozen
Doughnuts...66

Mock Macarons...69

Lollipop, Lollipop...71

Candy Buttons...74

Cupcake Cuties...77

Faux Cone
Snow Cone...79

A Slice of Pie...82

Lovely Little Layer Cakes

WITHOUT A DOUBT, *these Lovely Little Layer Cakes are one of my favorite projects in this entire book! They are ridiculously easy to make—you can use almost any soft cookie and frosting combo—and they taste incredible.*

Makes 6 cookie cakes

12 soft bakery cookies of your choice (I used Lofthouse® cookies, which come already frosted!)

1 (16-ounce) can frosting in color of your choice

½ cup sprinkles in color of your choice

1 (8.4-ounce) can Cloud White Betty Crocker® Decorating Cupcake Icing

1. Cut each cookie with a round cookie cutter (should be slightly smaller than the size of the cookies), creating twelve cookies that are all equal in size and shape. Set the leftover scraps aside.

There are so many options when making these little cakes. You can use red velvet cookies and cream cheese frosting, peanut butter cookies and choc-olate frosting, choco-late cookies and pecan frosting—the list just goes on and on! Some cookie brands are now making big, soft bakery-style cookies, so check your cookie aisle for more flavor combinations.

2. Place six of the cookies onto the plate or plates they will be served on. Spread frosting on the top of each of the six cookies.

3. Place an unfrosted cookie on top of each frosted cookie, facedown, with the top of the cookie facing the frosting.

4. Spread the frosting on the top and sides of each cookie cake.

5. Garnish the top of the cookie cakes with sprinkles or cookie crumbs from the leftover scraps that you set aside. Pipe decorative cupcake icing around the base of the cookie cakes.

We All Scream
for Ice Cream Cones

I LOVE ICE CREAM CONES. *They're obviously great for ice cream, but I also like to bake cake in them—a trick I learned from my friend Risa—and I even stack cookies on them. These ice cream cookie cones look just like soft serve ice cream cones. People are always amazed and wowed that they're not actually made with ice cream!*

Makes 8 cookie cones

32 soft chewy-style chocolate chip cookies

1 (16-ounce) can vanilla frosting

½ cup confectioners' sugar

8 ice cream cake cones

6 ounces chocolate candy coating

Rainbow sprinkles (about ¼ cup)

8 red gumballs

1. Use four graduated-size round cookie cutters from approximately 2 inches in diameter (the sizes are flexible; just make sure the largest cutter is slightly smaller than the cookies) to cut out eight cookies in each size, for a total of 32 cookies.

2. Scoop the frosting into a medium-size bowl. Add the confectioners' sugar to the frosting and mix well with a hand mixer or an electric mixer.

3. Fill a piping bag, a pastry bag, or a large zipper-style freezer bag with the frosting. If you're using a zipper-style bag, snip off a corner of the bag. The hole should be about ¼ inch wide.

4. Stand the ice cream cones up to prepare for the assembly. You can set the cones on a table or counter-top or, for added stability, set them in a cupcake tin or even in small cups.

5. With the piping bag, pipe a line of frosting around the top rim of one of the ice cream cones, and immediately place one of the 2-inch-wide cookies onto the top of the frosting-topped cone. Repeat with the remaining seven cones.

6. Add a dollop of frosting to the top of each cookie, and place a 1 ½-inch cookie on top of each.

7. Repeat the process with the 1-inch cookies and ½-inch cookies so that each cone has a total of four cookies stacked on top of it.

8. Once all the cones have stacks of cookies on them, pipe the remaining frosting around the stacks, swirling around from bottom to top, similar to how soft serve ice cream is swirled onto a cone.

9. Once all the cones are frosted, place them in the refrigerator for at least 1 hour.

10. Melt the candy coating according to package directions.

11. Working one cone at a time, drizzle a spoonful of chocolate coating on top of the cone, immediately adding a few sprinkles and topping with a gumball, before the chocolate coating dries. Repeat with each cone. Don't worry if some chocolate coating runs down the cones— that only adds to the look!

A Dozen Doughnuts

THESE DARLING LITTLE "DOUGHNUTS" *are made from sugar cookies! They look so realistic that you may just fool a few friends. With some sugar cookies, cookie cutters, and frosting and sprinkles, you can whip these doughnut cookies out in no time. Feel free to get creative, or even crazy, with your choice of toppings! Use whatever you love, from coconut to sprinkles to nuts to chocolate chips—the sky's the limit!*

Makes 12 cookies

12 soft sugar cookies

1 (16-ounce) can Duncan Hines® Creamy Home-Style Frosting in flavor of your choice

½ cup toppings, such as sprinkles, nuts, chocolate chips, or shredded coconut

SMART COOKIE TIP:

Many of the cookies in this book are perfect for gift-giving. These doughnut cookies, for example, would be perfect coupled with a gift card to the recipient's favorite coffee shop.

1. Cut twelve cookies with a doughnut cutter, or cut the centers out of each cookie with a small round cookie cutter. Place them on a baking sheet lined with waxed paper or parchment paper and set aside.

2. Place the frosting in a microwave-safe bowl, and heat for 10 seconds. Remove from the microwave and stir well. If the frosting is a consistency similar to syrup, it's ready to coat the cookies. If it's too thick, return it to the microwave for 5 additional seconds, and remove, stir, and repeat until the frosting has a syrup-like consistency.

3. Pour or spoon the melted frosting on top of a cookie. Immediately sprinkle with a generous layer of sprinkles, coconut, chopped nuts, or your topping of choice. Repeat with the remaining cookies.

Mock Macarons

MACARONS ARE ALL THE RAGE RIGHT NOW. *In addition to being delicious, they are truly adorable. These Mock Macarons have a similar sweet look, but are made with vanilla wafer cookies. You can make these in any color you want, and even flavor the frosting if you'd like. I left the filling in my version white, but feel free to use any color filling. Macarons add a great punch of color to a dessert buffet, and they look great displayed in clear glass jars, clear bags, or clear containers for gift-giving.*

Makes 16 cookies

32 vanilla wafers

2 (16-ounce) cans vanilla Duncan Hines® Creamy Home-Style Frosting

Food coloring in color of your choice

1. Place the vanilla wafers, top-side up, on a wire rack that is on a baking sheet lined with waxed or parchment paper.

2. Put 1½ cans of frosting into a microwave-safe bowl. Drop the food coloring into the frosting one to two drops at a time, stirring well after each drop. Continue adding more color until the desired shade is reached.

3. Put the frosting into the microwave and heat for 15 seconds. Remove from the microwave and stir well. The frosting should be the consistency of syrup. If the frosting is too thick, return it to the microwave for 5 seconds more, remove, and stir. Repeat this process until the frosting is the consistency of syrup.

4. Using a spoon, dollop the melted frosting over all the vanilla wafers until the tops of the wafers are completely covered in frosting. Excess frosting will run through the wire rack and onto the baking sheet beneath it. Let dry for at least 2 hours.

5. Place the remaining vanilla frosting into a piping bag or a large zipper-style freezer bag, pushing the frosting down into one corner of the bag. If you're using the zipper-style freezer bag, snip the corner end off the bag, creating an opening about 1/4 inch wide. Squeeze a small amount of the frosting onto the unfrosted side of sixteen cookies.

6. Place an unfrosted cookie on top of each to create a sandwich cookie.

Lollipop, Lollipop

I'M NOT SURE WHAT IT IS THAT MAKES *lollipops so much fun; they have some sort of magical quality. Even my pediatrician's office has a basket full of them for the kiddos as they leave. These lollipop cookies are fabulous for any occasion and are a hit with both kids and adults alike. And you can make these in any color to fit any theme.*

*Makes 12
cookie pops*

**12 ounces candy
coating in color of
your choice**

**12 round sandwich
cookies**

**12 lollipop sticks or
straws**

White candy writer

**White crystal sugar
or sanding sugar
(about ½ cup)**

1. Prepare candy coating according to package directions.

2. Carefully twist apart the sandwich cookies and lay them out on a baking sheet lined with waxed or parchment paper. Using a lollipop stick or straw, make an indentation in the filling of each cookie.

3. Dip the end of the lollipop stick or straw into the candy coating, covering about 1 inch of the stick in the candy coating, and then gently press it into the indentation in the filling.

4. Place 1 to 2 teaspoons of additional candy coating on top of the stick where it is pressed into the filling. Place the top of the cookie back on. Repeat with the remaining cookies, then carefully place them in the refrigerator to chill for at least 15 minutes.

5. Prepare the candy writer according to package directions.

6. If necessary, reheat the candy coating according to package directions. Working one cookie at a time, remove the cookie from the refrigerator and, holding it by the stick, dip the cookie into the candy coating, completely covering the cookie. Let excess candy coating drip off the cookie and back into the container.

7. Place the cookie on a baking sheet lined with waxed or parchment paper. Immediately use the candy writer. Starting at the center of the cookie, squeeze white candy coating from the candy writer onto the cookie and swirl in a circular motion.

These cookies look great packaged in clear, food-safe, cellophane bags and tied with ribbon, just like a lollipop!

8. Sprinkle with white crystal sugar or sanding sugar. Repeat with the remaining cookies. Let dry for at least 2 hours.

Candy Buttons

CANDY BUTTONS, OR DOTS, *are one of those candies that I remember fondly from my childhood. There was something so delightful about pulling those colorful little dots of sugar off their paper backing. These candy button cookies are a great way to re-create an old favorite. They would be perfect for a candy-themed birthday party, either served as a dessert or packaged as a party favor. To package these cookies, place a single cookie into a clear, food-safe, cellophane bag and tie the bag shut with colorful ribbon.*

Makes 12 cookies

12 graham cracker sheets

1 (7-ounce) pouch white Betty Crocker® Decorating Cookie Icing

12 strips candy dots

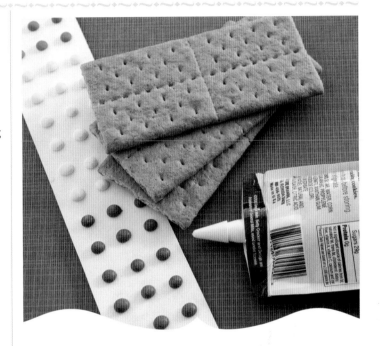

1. Lay out the twelve graham cracker sheets.

2. Prepare the cookie icing according to package directions.

3. Working one graham cracker at a time, squeeze the cookie icing onto a graham cracker, creating a rectangular shape in frosting. Immediately pull the candy dots off the paper backing and place them on the wet frosting, replicating the pattern of the candy dots on the paper. Repeat with the remaining cookies. Let dry for at least 4 hours.

Cupcake Cuties

YOU CAN'T HAVE A CHAPTER *about dessert and not include cupcakes! You can use any color candy coating that you prefer for the base of the cupcake, and you certainly are not limited to white for the frosting. While I used two different Pepperidge Farm® cookies to create my "cupcakes," you can use other brands as well. Find a rectangular- or square-shaped cookie for the base and a round cookie for the top. Get creative with the sprinkles and you could even add a birthday candle—just no lighting it!*

Makes 12 cookies

6 ounces candy coating in color(s) of your choice

12 Pepperidge Farm® shortbread cookies

12 Pepperidge Farm® coconut cookies

1 (8.4-ounce) can Cloud White Betty Crocker® Decorating Cupcake Icing

Sprinkles (about ¼ cup)

12 heart-shaped quins

1. Prepare the candy coating according to package directions. Line a baking sheet with waxed or parchment paper.

2. Working one cookie at a time, dip a Pepperidge Farm® shortbread cookie into the candy coating, completely covering the front of the cookie. Place the cookie on the waxed paper and immediately place a Pepperidge Farm® coconut cookie onto the cookie covered in candy coating, with the coconut cookie covering approximately half the shortbread cookie.

3. Repeat with the remaining cookies and allow to set until the candy coating is firm to the touch, at least 1 hour.

4. Prepare the cupcake icing according to package directions and select the decorating tip of your choice (a star tip works well).

5. Cover the coconut cookies with the cupcake frosting and finish with sprinkles and a decorative quin on the top of each cupcake cookie.

Faux Cone Snow Cone

MY OLDER DAUGHTER, *Bella, is a little obsessed with snow cones, especially blue raspberry snow cones. I thought it would be fun to turn her favorite dessert into a cookie, and when I found Wilton® Sugar Gems, it was very easy to do. Wilton® Sugar Gems are a lot like rock candy in a container! And they come in a variety of colors. Don't worry: If you can't find them, you can always use regular rock candy in their place. Just crush it a bit before placing it on the cookie: You want to make sure the pieces are bite-sized.*

Makes 12 cookies

12 half-sheet
graham crackers

6 ounces white
candy coating

12 Walkers shortbread
triangle cookies

½ (16-ounce) can
vanilla frosting

Food coloring in
pink, blue, or another
color of your choice
(optional)

Flavor extracts, such
as raspberry or cherry
(optional)

Wilton® Sugar Gems in
color(s) of your choice
(about ½ cup)

1. Use a round cookie cutter, approximately 2 inches in diameter, to cut the twelve top pieces for snow cones out of graham crackers. To do this, place the cookie cutter slightly off the edge of the graham cracker before cutting, as the shape should be flat, not round, on the bottom; it should resemble something between a half circle and a full circle shape.

2. Prepare the candy coating according to package directions.

3. Working one cookie at a time, dip the triangle cookie into the candy coating, covering the top and sides of the triangle with the coating.

I recommend using colored frosting under your rock candy. For fun, you can even add a few drops of raspberry-flavored extract.

4. Place the cookie on a baking sheet lined with waxed or parchment paper. Immediately place a cut graham cracker onto the top of the triangle to replicate the shape of a snow cone. Hold the graham cracker in place until the candy coating sets. Repeat with the remaining cookies.

5. Place the frosting in a bowl and, if desired, add food coloring, one drop at a time, stirring after each addition, until the desired shade is reached.

6. If you're flavoring the frosting, add one to two drops of raspberry or cherry extract and stir well to combine.

7. Frost the graham cracker portion of each cookie and sprinkle with Wilton® Sugar Gems. Let set for at least 1 hour.

A Slice of Pie

CAN I OFFER YOU A SLICE OF PIE? *A cute little cookie pie? Walkers shortbread triangle cookies are the perfect base for many different flavors. Coconut pecan frosting (shown in ramekin) makes for sweet little pecan pies, lemon frosting creates the look of lemon meringue, you can't go wrong with chocolate, and you can even use strawberry jam in place of frosting. Whatever your favorite frosting flavor is, it's guaranteed to work well on these cookies.*

Makes 12 cookies

12 Walkers shortbread triangle cookies

1 (16-ounce) can frosting of your choice

1 (8.4-ounce) can Cloud White Betty Crocker® Decorating Cupcake Icing

12 pieces garnish of your choice, such as pecans, chocolate chips, shredded coconut, chopped lemon candies, etc.

SMART COOKIE TIP:

I used white frosting to replicate the look of whipped cream, but if you're serving these cookies right after making them, you can use real whipped cream!

1. Spread the cookies with the frosting of your choice.

2. Pipe on white cupcake icing to replicate the look of whipped cream.

3. Garnish with candies, nuts, or other toppings of your choice.

CHAPTER 4

Happy Holidays

The holidays are always a great time
for baking and making edible gifts.
These fun and festive cookies are not
only sweet to eat, but they also make
for a great holiday centerpiece.

Happy Halloween
Pops ... 86

Along Came a Spider ... 92

Sweet Little Turkeys ... 95

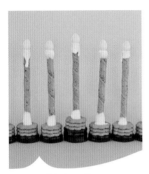

Light the
Menorah ... 97

O Christmas
Tree ... 100

Conversation
Hearts ... 102

Lucky Leprechaun
Hats ... 105

Little Bunny Pop Pops ... 109

Easter Baskets ... 111

You're a Grand
Old Flag ... 114

Happy Halloween Pops

I LOVE EVERYTHING ABOUT HALLOWEEN: *the decorating, the parties, the costumes—it's all so much fun. It's one of my favorite holidays to make treats for, which is why I created three different versions of my Halloween Pops. These cookie pops are very easy to make, and you can come up with so many different versions of them just by changing up the shape of the cookies you use and the colors and items you decorate them with.*

GHOST POPS

Makes 12 cookie pops

12 ounces white candy coating

12 Nutter Butter® cookies

12 lollipop sticks or straws

24 candy eyeballs

1. Prepare the white candy coating according to package directions.

2. Carefully twist apart the Nutter Butter® cookies and lay them out on a baking sheet lined with waxed or parchment paper.

3. Using a lollipop stick or straw, make an indentation in the filling of each cookie. Dip the end of the lollipop stick or straw into the candy coating, covering about 1 inch of the stick in the candy coating, and then gently press it into the indentation in the filling.

4. Place 1 to 2 teaspoons of additional candy coating on top of the stick where it is pressed into the filling. Place the top of the cookie back onto the cookie sandwich. Repeat with the remaining cookies. Carefully place them in the refrigerator to chill for at least 15 minutes.

5. If necessary, reheat the candy coating according to package directions. Working one cookie at a time, remove the cookie from the refrigerator and, holding it by the stick, dip the cookie into the candy coating, covering it completely. Let excess candy coating drip off the cookie and back into the container.

6. Place the cookie onto a baking sheet lined with waxed or parchment paper. Immediately place two candy eyeballs onto each candy coating-covered cookie. Repeat with the remaining cookies. Allow to dry for at least 1 hour.

MONSTER POPS

Makes 12 cookie pops

12 ounces light green candy coating (mix bright green and white candy coating if you cannot find light green)

12 rectangular-shaped sandwich cookies

12 lollipop sticks or straws

6 Tootsie Roll® Chocolate Midgees

24 candy eyeballs

Black candy writer

24 Kraft Jet-Puffed Mallow Bits

1. Prepare the light green candy coating according to package directions.

2. Carefully twist apart the sandwich cookies and lay them out on a baking sheet lined with waxed or parchment paper. For our purposes, the short sides of the cookies should be considered the top and bottom.

3. Using a lollipop stick or straw, make an indentation in the filling of each cookie. Dip the end of the lollipop stick or straw into the candy coating, covering about 1 inch of the stick in the candy coating, and then gently press it into the indentation in the filling.

4. Place 1 to 2 teaspoons of additional candy coating on top of the stick where it is pressed into the filling. Place the top of the cookie back onto the cookie sandwich. Repeat with the remaining cookies, then carefully place them in the refrigerator to chill for at least 15 minutes.

5. Unwrap the Tootsie Roll® Chocolate Midgees. Using a mini rolling pin, roll out the candies to roughly 1/4 inch in thickness to create the monster hair.

6. Using a small knife or cookie cutter, cut the candy into a rectangular shape the same width as the short side of the sandwich cookies. Cut out triangle shapes to create a jagged edge. Repeat the process to create twelve pieces of candy hair for the cookies.

7. If necessary, reheat the candy coating according to package directions. Working one cookie at a time, remove the cookie from the refrigerator and, holding it

by the stick, dip the cookie into the candy coating, covering the cookie completely. Let excess candy coating drip off the cookie and back into the container.

8. Place the cookie onto a baking sheet lined with waxed paper. Immediately place two candy eyeballs and the chocolate candy hair onto the cookie. Repeat with the remaining cookies and allow to dry for at least 1 hour.

9. Prepare the black candy writer according to package directions. Squeeze a small jagged line of black candy coating onto each cookie to create the monster's mouth.

10. Squeeze a dollop of black candy coating from the black candy writer onto one side of the cookie pop approximately halfway down the cookie, and immediately place a Jet-Puffed Mallow Bit onto the black candy coating as an ear. Hold the Mallow Bit in place until the candy coating starts to set. Repeat on the other side of the cookie, then place the cookie on the baking sheet lined with waxed paper. Repeat with the remaining cookies. Allow to dry for at least 2 hours.

JACK-O'-LANTERN POPS

Makes 12 cookie pops

12 ounces orange candy coating

12 round sandwich cookies

12 lollipop sticks or straws

3 Tootsie Roll® Chocolate Midgees

½ cup mini chocolate chips

Black candy writer

Rainbow sprinkles (about ¼ cup)

Black licorice laces (about 18 inches long), cut into 1½-inch-long segments

1. Prepare the orange candy coating according to package directions.

2. Carefully twist apart the sandwich cookies and lay them out on a baking sheet lined with waxed or parchment paper.

3. Using a lollipop stick or straw, make an indentation in the filling of each cookie. Dip the end of the lollipop stick or straw into the candy coating, covering about 1 inch of the stick in the candy coating, and then gently press it into the indentation in the filling.

4. Place 1 to 2 teaspoons of additional candy coating on top of the stick, where it is pressed into the filling. Place the top of the cookie back onto the cookie sandwich. Repeat with the remaining cookies. Carefully place them in the refrigerator to chill for at least 15 minutes.

5. Unwrap the Tootsie Roll® Chocolate Midgees. Using a mini rolling pin, roll out the candies to roughly ¼ inch in thickness. Using a small knife or cookie cutter, cut the candy into twenty-four small triangular shapes to create jack-o'-lantern eyes.

6. If necessary, reheat the candy coating according to package directions. Remove the cookies from the refrigerator. Working one cookie at a time, holding it by the stick, dip the cookie into the candy coating, covering each cookie completely. Let excess candy coating drip off the cookie and back into the container.

7. Place the cookie onto a baking sheet lined with waxed paper. Immediately place two chocolate triangle eyes onto the cookie and put mini chocolate chips on the cookie to create a nose and mouth. Repeat with the remaining cookies and allow to dry for at least 1 hour.

8. Prepare the black candy writer according to package directions. Squeeze a dollop of black candy coating, approximately the size of a penny, onto the top of a cookie pop. Sprinkle rainbow sprinkles over the candy coating. Squeeze two additional small dollops of black candy coating onto both sides of the rainbow sprinkles.

9. Place a piece of black licorice on top of the cookie, with the ends dipped in black candy coating so it creates a handle. Hold in place until the candy coating starts to set and can hold the licorice on its own. Place on the baking sheet lined with waxed paper. Repeat with the remaining cookies and allow to dry for at least 2 hours.

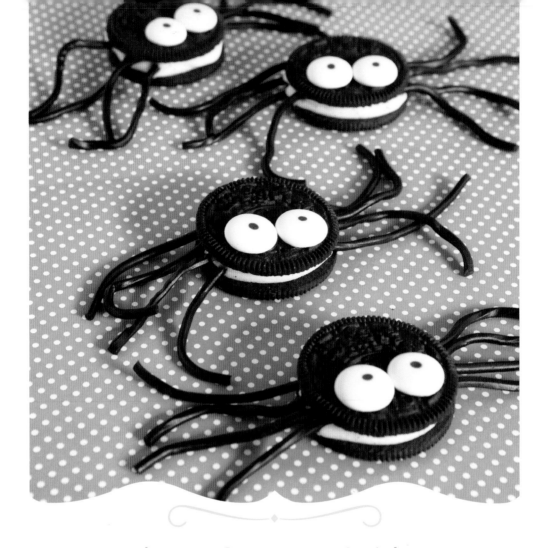

Along Came a Spider

NEED A SUPER-QUICK, SUPER-EASY *Halloween treat? Here you go! These spider cookies come together in no time at all. Twist open the chocolate sandwich cookies, add some black lace licorice strands and white candy coating, close up the cookies, and add the eyes—that's all it takes!*

Makes 12 cookies

Black licorice laces (about 16 feet long)

12 chocolate sandwich cookies

1 cup white candy coating

24 candy eyeballs

1. Cut the licorice into 48 strips, each approximately 4 inches in length.

2. Gently twist open the chocolate sandwich cookies.

3. Place four licorice strips onto the side of the sandwich cookie with the filling, and press gently into the filling.

4. Prepare the candy coating according to package directions. Working one cookie at a time, spoon approximately 1 to 2 teaspoons of the candy coating on top of the licorice strips and cookie filling. Place the top back on the sandwich cookie.

5. With a spoon, place a small amount of candy coating on top of the sandwich cookies where the spider eyes will be placed. Immediately place two candy eyeballs onto the candy coating. Repeat with the remaining cookies. Allow to dry for at least 2 hours.

Sweet Little Turkeys

NOT ONLY DO THESE LITTLE TURKEY *cookies make a sweet Thanksgiving treat, but they'd also look perfect on your dessert table or even at each and every place setting.*

Makes 10 cookies

White candy writer

Approximately 70 pieces candy corn

20 round chocolate sandwich cookies

6 ounces black candy coating

10 Nutter Butter® cookies

20 candy eyeballs

10 orange candy–coated sunflower seeds

1. Prepare the white candy writer according to package directions.

2. Squeeze a generous dollop of white candy coating from the candy writer onto the small end of a piece of candy corn. Working one cookie at a time, gently press the candy coating-covered end of the candy corn into a round sandwich cookie, pressing between the two halves of the cookie, into the filling.

3. Repeat with six more pieces of candy corn, resulting in half the cookie having candy corn pieces sticking out to replicate turkey feathers. Repeat with nine additional sandwich cookies.

4. Allow the candy coating to set for at least 1 hour.

5. Prepare the black candy coating according to package directions. Spoon approximately 2 teaspoons of the coating onto the front of one sandwich cookie with attached candy corns.

6. Gently press one Nutter Butter® cookie onto the black candy coating–topped cookie to create the body of the turkey. Repeat with the remaining Nutter Butter® cookies. Allow the candy coating to set for at least 30 minutes.

7. If necessary, reheat the black candy coating according to package directions. Place approximately 2 teaspoons of black candy coating onto one of the remaining sandwich cookies.

8. Gently place a cookie turkey body upright onto the candy coating and hold it in place until the candy coating starts to set, approximately 1 minute. Repeat with the remaining nine sandwich cookies and cookie turkey bodies. Allow the candy coating to set for at least 30 minutes.

9. Prepare the white candy writer according to package directions. Place three small dots of candy coating onto the front face area of a Nutter Butter® cookie, where the eyes and a nose would be placed.

10. Gently press two candy eyes and an orange candy-coated sunflower seed onto the candy coating to create the turkey's face. Repeat with the remaining cookies, candy eyeballs, and sunflower seeds. Allow to dry for at least 1 hour.

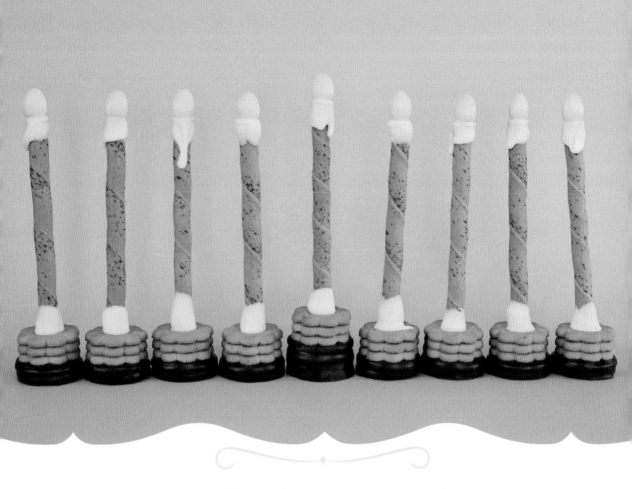

Light the Menorah

THIS COOKIE MENORAH IS SUCH A FUN TREAT *to make for Hanukkah! Made with Murray Sugar Free® shortbread cookies, Pepperidge Farm® Pirouette® rolled wafer cookies, and Oreo® cookies, it is quite tasty, in addition to being cute. You can always substitute pretzel rods for the rolled wafer cookies, if you'd like, and yellow peanut M&M's® can be used in place of Jordan almonds.*

Makes 9 cookie candles

Wilton® Dab-N-Hold™ edible adhesive

27 Murray Sugar Free® shortbread cookies

6 ounces white candy coating

9 Pepperidge Farm® Pirouette® rolled wafer cookies

9 yellow Jordan almonds

White candy writer

6 ounces blue candy coating

10 round sandwich cookies

1. Place four to five drops of Wilton® Dab-N-Hold™ edible adhesive onto the top of a Murray Sugar Free® shortbread cookie, and place a second cookie on top.

2. Place four to five drops of the edible adhesive on top of the second cookie, and place a third cookie on top, creating a small tower of three cookies. Repeat with the remaining cookies, creating eight towers of three cookies each. Allow to dry for at least 4 hours.

3. Prepare the white candy coating according to package directions. Working one cookie at a time, dip one end of a Pirouette® into the white candy coating, and immediately place a Jordan almond on top of the white candy coating while it's still wet.

4. Hold the Jordan almond in place until the candy coating starts to set. It's okay if the candy coating drips down the cookie; this will just make it look more like a real candle.

SMART COOKIE TIP:

Because these pretty candle cookies are a bit fragile, it wouldn't hurt to make one or two extras to have on hand, just in case!

5. Prepare a white candy writer according to package directions and squeeze some additional white candy coating on to create the candle effect. Once the candy coating is set, lay the Pirouette® cookies onto a baking sheet lined with waxed or parchment paper.

6. Prepare the blue candy coating according to package directions. Working one cookie at a time, dip the sandwich cookie into the blue candy coating, then place the cookie on a baking sheet lined with waxed or parchment paper. (I like working with my hands, but feel free to use small tongs or clean tweezers for this step if that's easier for you. Just be super careful so the cookies don't break!)

7. Immediately place a shortbread cookie stack on top of the blue candy coating–covered sandwich cookie. Repeat with seven more sandwich cookies. The final two sandwich cookies will be used together to create a double-height cookie.

8. Dip one sandwich cookie into the blue candy coating and place it on waxed paper, then immediately dip the last cookie into the candy coating and place it on top of the first cookie. Top both cookies with the final shortbread cookie stack. Allow to dry for at least 1 hour.

9. If necessary, reheat the white candy coating according to package directions. Let the candy coating cool slightly, as a thickened, slightly cooled coating will work best. Dip the end of a Pirouette® cookie into the candy coating, covering about 1 inch, then immediately place the Pirouette® onto one of the shortbread cookie stacks. Hold in place until the candy coating sets and the cookie can stand on its own. Repeat with the remaining cookies. These cookies are fragile, so handle with care.

O Christmas Tree

THERE IS SO MUCH TO LOVE about these Christmas tree cookies. They are simple to make, take very little time to decorate, and are delicious. One of my favorite things about them is that they are 3D, giving some nice height to your cookie platter or dessert table. I prefer to cover mine in white or green frosting and then cover with a simple white sugar. For a fun and whimsical feel, cover them in candies and sprinkles and get creative! You can create a lovely holiday centerpiece by displaying these cookies on a bed of sugar—to mimic snow—or on top of a platter or cake stand.

Makes 12 cookies

1 (16-ounce) can
white frosting

Green food coloring

12 round cookies,
slightly larger than
the widest part of the
sugar cones

12 sugar cones

1 cup of your favorite
sprinkles, candies, or
sugars, for decorating

SMART COOKIE TIP:
Experiment with different
colors for these Christmas
trees and you can easily
create black witches' hats
for Halloween or even
blue wizards' hats.

1. To make green frosting, place the white frosting in a
   bowl and add the green food coloring one drop at a
   time, stirring after each addition. Continue adding color
   and stirring until the desired shade is reached.

2. Spread the cookies with a layer of frosting.

3. Place one sugar cone on each cookie. Ice the sugar
   cones with frosting. Add sprinkles, candies, or decorations as desired.

Conversation Hearts

THE FIRST CANDIES I THINK OF *when I think of Valentine's Day are conversation hearts. While I've always loved the concept of conversation hearts, I've never really liked actually eating them. These cookies have the same look as conversation hearts, but in new and bright colors—and they taste amazing! You can use any heart-shaped cookies or cut your own heart shapes out of soft cookies with a cookie cutter, but the Walkers shortbreads are light, buttery, and delightful.*

Makes 12 cookies

12 Walkers shortbread hearts cookies

1 (16-ounce) can vanilla Duncan Hines® Creamy Home-Style Frosting, divided

Food coloring in color(s) of your choice

Sanding sugar(s) in color(s) of your choice (about ½ cup)

White candy writer (optional)

1. Place the cookies on a wire rack on top of a baking sheet lined with waxed or parchment paper.

Sanding sugar works well on these cookies, giving them a nice decorative look and a surface that you can still write on. Feel free to write fun messages or even personalize them with names. While I used bright colors, you can use any colors that you'd like, from pastels to dark reds. Your sweethearts will love them! Also, these little heart cookies would be super-cute as cupcake toppers!

2. Place 1¾ cups of the frosting into a microwave-safe bowl, reserving the last ¼ cup for later. Put the frosting in the microwave and heat for 10 seconds. Remove from the microwave and stir well. If the frosting is a consistency similar to syrup, it's ready to coat the cookies. If it's too thick, return it to the microwave for 5 additional seconds, remove, stir, and repeat until the frosting has a consistency like syrup.

3. Add food coloring, one drop at a time, stirring well after each addition, until the desired shade is reached. Pour or spoon melted frosting over the cookies. Excess frosting will drip onto the baking sheet. Immediately sprinkle the cookies with sanding sugar. Allow to dry for at least 1 hour.

4. Place the remaining ¼ cup of vanilla frosting into a piping bag or a large zipper-style freezer bag, with frosting pressed down into one corner of the bag. If you're using a zipper-style freezer bag, snip off a corner of the bag to create a very small hole, less than ⅛ inch wide. Write on the cookies by squeezing icing onto them. (You could also use a white candy writer—whichever is easier for you.)

Lucky Leprechaun Hats

I ALWAYS ENJOY ST. PATRICK'S DAY. *I'm not sure if it's my Irish heritage or because for years my daughter really thought that leprechauns showed up on St. Patrick's Day to play tricks on everyone! Either way, it's fun to celebrate, and these Lucky Leprechaun Hats are a tasty way to do just that.*

Makes 12 cookies

12 ounces green candy coating

12 Joy® Mini Cups ice cream cones

Green crystal sugar sprinkles (about ½ cup)

12 Keebler® Fudge Stripes™ dark chocolate cookies

8 ounces chocolate candy coating

12 pieces yellow Chiclets gum squares

1. Prepare the green candy coating according to package directions. Working one ice cream cone at a time, dip the bottom portion of the cone into the green candy coating, letting excess coating drip off into the dipping bowl.

SMART COOKIE TIP:

To make pilgrim hats for Thanksgiving, you can use all chocolate candy coating, or replace the green candy coating with white.

2. Sprinkle the candy coating–covered area with green crystal sugar sprinkles. Place on a baking sheet lined with waxed paper, with the uncoated side of the cone touching the paper. Repeat with the remaining cones. Allow to dry for at least 1 hour.

3. Lay the Fudge Stripes™ cookies on a baking sheet lined with waxed or parchment paper.

4. Prepare the chocolate candy coating according to package directions. Using a toothpick, place a small dot of chocolate candy coating onto the center of each yellow Chiclet square. Allow to set for at least 15 minutes.

5. Working one cone at a time, dip the uncoated part of the cone into the chocolate candy coating, letting excess coating drip into the dipping bowl. Immediately place the freshly dipped area of the cone onto the center of a Fudge Stripes™ cookie to create the hat.

6. Place a yellow Chiclet square on the front center of the chocolate candy coating area of the cone. Hold in place with your finger until the chocolate candy coating starts to set and will hold on its own. Repeat with the remaining cookies. Allow to dry for at least 2 hours.

Little Bunny Pop Pops

These funny little bunny pops make a sweet treat for your Easter activities. They are created with round sandwich cookies, candy coating, candies, sprinkles, and Jordan almonds. While the Jordan almonds are a perfect shape for the bunny ears, feel free to use peanut M&M's® or any other similar-shaped candy in their place. You can also use chocolate coating if you prefer a chocolate Easter bunny.

Makes 12 cookie pops

24 Jordan almonds

12 ounces white candy coating

12 round sandwich cookies

12 lollipop sticks or straws

24 small candy eyeballs

12 pink SweetWorks® Pearls™

12 miniature marshmallows, each cut in half widthwise

12 pink heart quins

1. Place the almonds in the freezer.

2. Prepare the candy coating according to package directions. Carefully twist apart the sandwich cookies and lay them on a baking sheet lined with waxed or parchment paper.

SMART COOKIE TIP:

I love to use decorative paper party straws when I make cookie pops. While white lollipop sticks certainly serve the purpose, party straws come in every color and pattern you can imagine and can add even more fun and whimsy to your pops.

3. Using a lollipop stick or straw, make an indentation in the filling of each cookie. Dip the end of the lollipop stick or straw into the candy coating, covering about 1 inch of the stick in the candy coating, and then gently press it into the indentation in the filling.

4. Place 1 to 2 teaspoons of additional candy coating onto the top of the stick where it is pressed into the filling. Place the top of the cookie back onto the sandwich cookie. Repeat with the remaining cookies and place them in the refrigerator for at least 30 minutes.

5. If necessary, reheat the candy coating according to package directions. Working one cookie at a time, remove the cookie from the refrigerator and two almonds from the freezer. Dip the bottom half of the almond into the candy coating and then immediately place it on the top right or left of the cookie pop, to create an ear. Hold it in place until the candy coating sets, approximately 30 seconds to 1 minute. Repeat with the second almond.

6. Once both almond ears are attached to the cookie, gently return it to the refrigerator. Repeat with the remaining cookies and almonds.

7. Remove a cookie pop with ears from the refrigerator and carefully dip or spoon candy coating over it.

8. Place the cookie pop on a baking sheet lined with waxed or parchment paper. Place two candy eyeballs on the bunny face, followed by a pink Pearl™ for the nose, two miniature marshmallow halves to create cheeks, and an upside down heart quin as a mouth. Repeat with the remaining cookies. Allow to dry for at least 2 hours.

Easter Baskets

MY MOM ALWAYS PUT SO MUCH THOUGHT *into creating Easter baskets for my brother and me when we were kids. One item that has been an Easter basket staple my entire life: Marshmallow PEEPS®. Those sweet little sugar-colored marshmallows are a favorite of mine. These cute cookies can be set out on a holiday table for decoration or even used as placecard holders. For gift-giving, place these cookies in a clear box or a food-safe cellophane bag tied with decorative ribbon. These are fragile cookies, so handle them with care.*

Makes 12 cookies

36 pieces of Twizzlers Rainbow Twists licorice (about 12 inches each)

Candy writer in color of your choice

12 sugar cookies

2 cups shredded coconut

Green food coloring

12 Marshmallow PEEPS®

24 jelly beans

¼ cup rainbow sprinkles

1. Create circle shapes with twenty-four pieces of licorice and secure the ends with a clean, dry clothespin to hold the circle shape in place. Let them sit for 24 hours to set, then remove the clothespins.

2. Prepare the candy writer according to package directions. Squeeze the candy coating from the candy writer onto the bottom of a round piece of licorice and place the licorice on a sugar cookie. Repeat with the remaining eleven cookies.

3. Squeeze the candy coating from the candy writer onto another round piece of licorice and place on top of a round piece of licorice already on a cookie, creating a basket that is two pieces high. Repeat with the remaining round licorice pieces.

SMART COOKIE TIP:

You can use colored sanding sugars to help cover up the white marshmallow that is left exposed when you separate the Marshmallow PEEPS®. Simply dip the exposed marshmallow area of the PEEPS® into colored sanding sugar immediately after you separate your PEEPS®. The marshmallow is sticky enough for the sugar to stick right to it.

4. Put the shredded coconut and two to three drops of green food coloring in a large zipper-style freezer bag. Close the bag tightly and shake well to combine. Once it's thoroughly combined, sprinkle a small amount of coconut into the center of each licorice basket.

5. Set a Marshmallow PEEPS® chick into each basket on top of the colored coconut.

6. Using the candy writer, place two generous dots of candy coating onto the top sides of a licorice basket and on the ends of a piece of licorice. Then place the licorice on top of the basket, to create a handle. Hold in place until the candy coating has set (or use clothespins to prop the handle into place). Repeat with the remaining baskets and licorice.

7. Use the candy writer to place a small amount of candy coating on the back of the jelly beans, and place two jelly beans next to the base of the handle on each basket, one on each side. Finish with a dusting of rainbow sprinkles.

You're a Grand Old Flag

THIS FUN FLAG COOKIE *is sure to be a hit at your Fourth of July gatherings. This recipe creates one flag, but feel free to double or triple the recipe to create more flags as needed. The Pirouette® cookies are arranged together to create the flag, but as the pieces will not be stuck together, each cookie can easily be picked up to eat and enjoy. For a salty alternative, you can create your flag with large pretzel rods instead of Pirouette® cookies.*

Makes 1 cookie

6 Pepperidge Farm® Pirouette® cookies

½ cup red candy coating

½ cup white candy coating

¼ cup blue candy coating

White nonpareils or mini pearl sprinkles

SMART COOKIE TIP:

When dipping the Pirouette® cookies into coating, I like working with my hands, but feel free to use small tongs or clean tweezers if that's easier for you. Just be super careful so the cookies don't break!

1. Chill the cookies in the freezer for at least 15 minutes.

2. Prepare the red and white candy coatings, in separate bowls, according to package directions. Line a baking sheet with waxed or parchment paper. Dip one Pirouette® cookie into the red candy coating, completely covering the cookie. Put it on the waxed paper.

3. Dip two more cookies partially into the red candy coating, covering approximately two thirds of each cookie in coating. Place them on the waxed paper to dry. Dip two cookies in white candy coating, completely covering each cookie. Place them on the waxed paper.

4. Dip one additional cookie partially in white coating, covering approximately two thirds of the cookie in coating. Put it on the waxed paper to dry.

5. Once the red and white candy coatings are dry to the touch, prepare the blue candy coating. Dip the uncovered parts of the cookies into the blue candy coating, place on the waxed paper, and garnish with white nonpareils or sprinkles. Allow to dry for at least 2 hours.

CHAPTER 5

Celebrate
Good Times

This chapter is all about celebrating the
special moments of life, from babies to
birthdays, graduations to weddings.
Many of these cookies make fabulous
party favors, so don't hesitate to package
some up and send your guests home
with a memorable sweet treat.

Birthday Balloons... *118*

Put On Your Party Hat... *120*

Congrats,
Graduate!... *122*

Engagement
Ring Bling... *125*

Wonderful
Wedding Cakes... *129*

Then Comes the Baby Carriage... *133*

Big Reveal Baby Rattles... *135*

Birthday Balloons

COOKIE POPS ARE TRULY EASY TO MAKE. *They are much easier and quicker than cake pops and there is no baking involved. You can make these fun birthday balloon cookie pops in any color to fit any theme or occasion. For birthdays, I love to use Oreo® Birthday Cake cookies, but any round, sandwich-style cookie will work just fine. I matched the color of my sanding sugar to the color of my candy coating to make these, but you can always stick to white candy coating and add the color with your sugars. Some of the white will show through the sugar, but you will still have adorable balloons that your friends and family will enjoy.*

Makes 12
cookie pops

**12 round sandwich
cookies**

**12 ounces candy
coating in color(s) of
your choice**

12 lollipop sticks

**½ cup sanding sugar in
color(s) of your choice**

White candy writer

1. Twist open the twelve sandwich cookies and place them on a baking sheet lined with waxed or parchment paper.

2. Prepare the candy coating according to package directions. Using a lollipop stick, make an indentation in the filling of each cookie. Dip the end of the stick into the candy coating, covering about 1 inch, then gently press it into the indentation. Repeat with the remaining cookies.

3. With a spoon, place approximately 1 to 2 teaspoons of the candy coating on top of the stick where it is pressed into the filling and immediately place the other half of the cookie on top of the coating. Repeat with the remaining cookies. Put the cookies in the refrigerator for at least 1 hour.

4. Reheat the candy coating according to package directions. One cookie at a time, dip the cookie into the candy coating, place on a baking sheet lined with waxed paper, and sprinkle the top with sanding sugar. Repeat with the remaining cookies and allow to set for at least 1 hour.

5. Prepare the candy writer according to package directions. Draw a small white highlight on the upper corner of each cookie. Allow to dry until firm to the touch, at least 1 hour.

Put On Your Party Hat

IT'S TIME TO PUT ON YOUR PARTY HAT *and sing "Happy Birthday"! You can easily match the colors on these hats to your party theme, or even switch up the colors to create witches' hats for Halloween or party hats for New Year's Eve. These fun hat cookies are so easy to make that you can even get the kids involved and let them make their own, a great activity to help keep them busy while you prepare other items for your party. I used Walkers shortbread triangle cookies, but any triangle-shaped cookie will do. If you can't find triangle cookies, you can always get soft sugar cookies and cut them into triangles with a cookie cutter or knife.*

Makes 15 cookies

1 (16-ounce) can frosting in color of your choice

Food coloring in color of your choice

15 Walkers shortbread triangle cookies

75 SweetWorks® Sixlets®

1 cup SweetWorks® Pearls™

15 small gumballs in color of your choice

1. Place the frosting in a medium-size bowl and add food coloring one drop at a time, stirring after each addition, until the desired shade is reached.

2. Frost each cookie.

3. Use about five SweetWorks® Sixlets® and a few Pearls™ to decorate each hat, then place a gumball at the top of each cookie.

SMART COOKIE TIP: Cookie decorating is one of my favorite activities to do at parties with kids, and these cookies are perfect for that. Kids of all ages love to decorate cookies; it brings out their creativity and you can work it into any theme or holiday. Small disposable condiment cups, which can be found at most grocery stores, are perfect for holding just enough frosting, sprinkles, or candies to decorate two or three cookies. Dull plastic knives, or even spoons for younger kids, are the perfect tools for applying frosting.

Congrats, Graduate!

GRADUATION IS SUCH A BIG DAY *and a cause for celebration. These sweet cookies are a perfect way to tell graduates what a great job they've done. You can substitute the SweetWorks® Sixlets® colors as well as the colors of the candy stars to match your graduate's school colors.*

Makes 12 graduation cap cookies and 12 diploma cookies

12 round chocolate sandwich cookies

12 ounces chocolate candy coating

12 half-sheet graham crackers

6 Pepperidge Farm® Pirouette® cookies

6 ounces white candy coating

48 candy stars (about ½ inch in diameter)

Black sanding sugar (about ½ cup)

Red licorice laces (about 72 inches long), cut into 2-inch-long segments

12 SweetWorks® Sixlets® in color of your choice

1. Place the chocolate sandwich cookies on a baking sheet lined with waxed or parchment paper.

2. Prepare the chocolate candy coating according to package directions. Place approximately 1 to 2 teaspoons of the candy coating on each sandwich cookie, and immediately place a graham cracker square on top of the sandwich cookie to create the graduation cap. Once all graduation caps are made, place them in the refrigerator to chill for at least 15 minutes.

3. Gently cut each Pirouette® cookie in half and brush off any crumbs.

4. Prepare the white candy coating according to package directions. Working one cookie at a time, dip a cut Pirouette® cookie into the white candy coating, covering it completely. (I like working with my hands, but

feel free to use small tongs or clean tweezers for this step if that's easier for you. Just be extremely gentle so the cookies don't break. It's a good idea to have a few extras on hand as back-up.)

5. Place the dipped cookie onto a baking sheet lined with waxed or parchment paper, and place three star candies in a row on top. Hold the stars in place for a few seconds while the coating starts to set. Repeat with the remaining Pirouette® cookies.

6. If necessary, reheat the chocolate candy coating according to package directions. Remove one graduation hat cookie at a time from the refrigerator and dip the graham cracker portion of the graduation cap into the candy coating. (The sandwich cookie does not need to be covered in chocolate candy coating.)

7. Immediately place the graduation cap cookie onto a baking sheet lined with waxed or parchment paper, and sprinkle the top of the cookie with black sanding sugar.

8. Add a small drop of chocolate candy coating to the top center of the graduation cap cookie. Press three red licorice strips into the chocolate candy coating on the top center of the cookie, allowing the ends to dangle off the side of the cookie.

9. Press a candy star into the top of the cookie, next to the licorice strips.

10. Place a dab of candy coating onto the bottom of a Sixlet® and place it on top of the candy star, holding it in place until the chocolate starts to set. Repeat with the remaining cookies.

Engagement Ring Bling

IT'S ALWAYS FUN TO COME UP WITH *a unique way to celebrate two people deciding to get married, and these fun engagement ring cookies do just that! These cookies are perfect for an engagement party or even to let friends and family know to save the date and that a wedding is on the way!*

ENGAGEMENT RING COOKIES

Makes 12 cookies

1 (16-ounce) can white frosting

Food coloring in color of your choice

12 square or rectangle-shaped cookies or graham cracker sheets

12 Murray Sugar Free® shortbread cookies, round flower shape

¼ cup corn syrup

¼ cup gold sanding sugar or crystal sugar

12 Hershey's Kisses®, kept in silver wrapping

1. Scoop approximately one fourth of the can of white frosting into a small bowl. Add food coloring as desired to create the accent color of your choice. Mix until well combined.

2. Place colored frosting into a decorating bag fitted with a small round piping tip, or into a large zipper-style freezer bag and cut off a bottom corner, leaving a hole approximately 1/8 inch wide.

3. Pipe a colored frosting outline onto each of the twelve square or rectangle cookies.

4. Place the remaining white frosting into a separate piping bag, fitted with a medium round piping tip, or into a large zipper-style freezer bag, and cut off a bottom corner, leaving a hole approximately 1/4 inch wide.

5. Pipe white frosting onto the cookies, filling in the area inside the colored outline.

6. Place the flower-shaped cookies on a sheet of waxed or parchment paper.

7. Working one cookie at a time, use a small craft paint brush to brush a thin layer of corn syrup onto the top of a flower-shaped cookie, and immediately sprinkle it with gold sanding sugar or crystal sugar. Gently place the cookie covered in sugar onto the white area of the frosted cookie.

8. Place a Hershey's Kiss® above the gold cookie to replicate the look of a ring. Repeat with the remaining cookies.

SAVE-THE-DATE COOKIES

Makes 12 cookies

1 (16-ounce) container white frosting

Food coloring in color of your choice

12 square or rectangle-shaped cookies or graham cracker sheets

12 round candies (such as Mentos® Chewy Mints)

1. Scoop out about ¼ cup of white frosting from the container and set aside.

2. Add food coloring as desired to create the accent color of your choice. Frost all the cookies with the colored frosting.

3. Place the remaining white frosting into a piping bag fitted with a fine round tip. Pipe lines of white frosting onto the frosted cookies to replicate the look of a calendar. Pipe the month and year onto the top of each cookie. Place one round candy onto each cookie, then pipe the date onto the round candy.

SMART COOKIE TIP:

I often find a variety of different cookie shapes in my grocery store bakery. The rectangle-shaped cookies I used in this project were found there. The cookies I used for this project featured a heart design but were the shape I wanted, so I simply covered up the design with my frosting. When you look beyond the themes, you can find some great cookie shapes and sizes.

Wonderful Wedding Cakes

MY FAVORITE PART OF ALMOST ANY WEDDING *is the cake! These wedding cake cookies are easy to make and are adorable. Cutting soft cookies into different-size circles, stacking them, and pouring melted frosting over them, creates perfect little wedding cakes. Using a candy writer, you can attach candy or sprinkles for embellishment.*

Makes 1 wedding cake cookie

6 large, soft round sugar cookies

White candy writer

1 (16-ounce) can vanilla Duncan Hines® Creamy Home-Style Frosting

SweetWorks® Pearls™ in color of your choice (about ½ cup)

Candy heart in color of your choice

1. Using round cookie cutters, cut the cookies into graduated sizes. Cut into two large, two medium, and two small cookies.

2. Prepare the candy writer according to package directions.

3. Place one large cookie on a wire rack on a baking sheet lined with waxed or parchment paper. Squeeze a small amount of the candy coating from the candy writer on top of the large cookie, about the size of a nickel. Immediately place the other large cookie on top. Repeat this process with the medium and small cookies, stacking largest to smallest, with candy coating between each layer.

These wedding cake cookies would be cute as cake toppers on top of a cake at a bridal shower, used as placecard holders, or given out as wedding favors. I love to place them in clear, food-safe, cellophane bags or in food-safe boxes. Cookies this pretty do not need a lot of extra decoration when they are packaged. They are so simple to create and you can use them in so many ways!

4. Place the frosting in a microwave-safe bowl. Put it in the microwave and heat for 10 seconds. Remove from the microwave and stir well. If the frosting is a consistency similar to syrup, it is ready to coat the cookies. If it's too thick, return it to the microwave for 5 additional seconds, remove, stir, and repeat until the frosting has a syruplike consistency.

5. Pour the frosting over the stacked cookies, completely covering the top and sides of the cookies. Excess frosting will drip down onto the baking sheet. Allow the cookie to dry for at least 4 hours. Once dry, use an offset spatula to very gently loosen the cookie from the wire rack, since the frosting will likely make the cookie stick to the rack. Transfer the cookie to the surface that you plan to display or serve it on.

6. Once again, prepare the candy writer according to package directions. Squeeze candy coating from the candy writer around one third of the base of the bottom cookie, and gently press Pearls™ into the coating.

7. Squeeze more candy coating onto the base of the cookie, pressing Pearls™ into the candy coating until the entire base is surrounded with a ring of Pearls™. Repeat with the medium and small layers.

8. Squeeze a small amount of candy coating onto the base of a heart candy, and gently place the heart on top of the cookie stack to replicate a cake topper. Allow to dry for at least 2 hours.

Then Comes the Baby Carriage

THESE COOKIES MIGHT JUST BE THE SWEETEST *part of your next baby shower! The baby carriage shape is easily created by using a soft round cookie and a square cookie cutter. Those sweet little baby faces are made from mini vanilla wafers, candy necklace beads, quin sprinkles, and an edible marker. You can go with pink, blue, or yellow frosting, or coordinate the frosting to match a special shower color. I used white Life Savers® Mints for the wheels on the cookies, but feel free to use any Life Saver® or other round candies that work for you.*

Makes 12 cookies

12 soft sugar cookies

1 (16-ounce) can frosting in color of your choice

½ cup white sanding sugar or crystal sugar

24 Life Savers® Mints

12 mini vanilla wafers

Black edible marker

Wilton® Dab-N-Hold™ edible adhesive

24 pink quins

12 candy necklace pieces

12 sugar pearls

Candy writer in a color that matches the frosting

1. Using a square cookie cutter, cut out the upper top right corner from each sugar cookie, creating the baby carriage shape.

2. Spread each cookie with frosting and sprinkle with sanding sugar or crystal sugar.

3. Press two Life Savers® Mints into the bottom of each cookie to create the carriage wheels.

4. To create the baby faces with the vanilla wafers, use a black edible marker to draw hair and eyes onto the vanilla wafers.

5. Using Wilton® Dab-N-Hold™, place two dots of edible adhesive on a vanilla wafer and place two pink quins on the dots to create cheeks. Repeat with the remaining faces.

6. Place a generous dot of edible adhesive for the mouth, and affix a candy necklace piece to create the base of a pacifier. Repeat with the remaining faces.

7. To each face, add a dot of edible adhesive to the top of the candy necklace piece and place a sugar pearl on it, finishing the pacifier. Allow the baby face cookies to dry for at least 6 hours.

8. Once the baby face cookies are dry and the adhesive has set, prepare the candy writer according to package directions. Squeeze a small amount of the candy coating from the writer on the cut-out portion of the baby carriage cookie.

9. Immediately place a baby face cookie on the carriage cookie, making sure that the two edges of the baby face cookie are placed against the candy coating. Hold the baby face cookie in place until the coating is set. Repeat with the remaining cookies.

Big Reveal Baby Rattles

GENDER REVEAL PARTIES ARE ALL THE RAGE *these days. It's fun to find a clever way to share the big news. These baby rattle cookies are the perfect way to tell friends and family that "It's a boy!" or "It's a girl!" By replacing the cookie filling with pink or blue candy coating, the gender surprise will be revealed when guests bite into these cute little rattle cookies. Not quite ready to spill the beans? That's okay, too; you can skip the secret centers altogether and still have adorable cookies that are perfect for baby showers.*

Makes 12 cookies

12 round sandwich cookies

12 lollipops

4 ounces pink or blue candy coating

12 ounces yellow candy coating

12 baby-themed sugar decorations

White candy writer

144 white sugar pearls

1. Twist open the sandwich cookies, scrape out the filling and lay the cookies on a baking sheet lined with waxed or parchment paper.

2. Lay the stick end of a lollipop onto a cookie. Repeat with the remaining cookies and lollipops.

3. Prepare the pink or blue candy coating according to package directions. One cookie at a time, place approximately 1 to 2 teaspoons of candy coating over the lollipop stick, then immediately set the other half of the cookie on top, putting the sandwich cookie back together with the stick inside. Repeat with the remaining cookies. Allow to set for 30 minutes.

4. Prepare the yellow candy coating according to package directions. Dip the cookie portion of a rattle into the yellow candy coating.

SMART COOKIE TIP:

To decorate my rattles, I used fun, baby-themed sugar decorations, which can be found in baking aisles, craft stores, and party supply stores. You certainly aren't limited to using these to decorate your rattles; sprinkles and candies work wonderfully as well. It's easier to work with these cookies if you leave the wrappers on the lollipops, taking the wrappers off just before displaying the cookies.

5. Place the cookie rattle onto waxed paper, and place a sugar decoration on top of the cookie before the candy coating has a chance to set. Repeat with the remaining cookies.

6. Once the candy coating is set and dry to the touch, prepare the candy writer according to package directions. Use the candy writer to create twelve dots of candy coating all around the edge of the front of a cookie, and immediately place a sugar pearl on each candy-coating dot.

7. Repeat with the remaining rattles. Let set until the candy coating is dry and all pearls are firmly attached to the cookies.

CHAPTER 6

Child's Play

This chapter is full of fun stuff
for the kids (kids of any age!).
If your favorite kiddos are always
busy with sports, dance, band,
and school, you'll find lots of great
treats in here that are perfect for them.

Play Ball... *140*

Beautiful Ballerinas... *144*

Star Student... *146*

Goody Goody Gumballs... *149*

Mr. Robot... *152*

Pretty Princess Wands... *154*

Smart Cookie... *157*

Making Music... *158*

Play Ball

FROM FOUR-YEAR-OLDS PLAYING TEE BALL, *to basketball in the park, to high school football, at some point almost all of us end up watching, playing, or cheering for sports teams. With team tryouts, big games, and end-of-season parties, there are loads of chances to celebrate. These sports cookies are just a few of the styles you can make. You can easily switch things up and create tennis balls, volleyballs, and soccer balls, just by changing the colors and detailing. These cookies would be fun personalized with team or player names, or player numbers. Just use a candy writer or frosting to personalize them.*

FOOTBALL COOKIES

Makes 12 cookies

12 football-shaped cookies

1 (16-ounce) can chocolate frosting

½ cup vanilla frosting

SMART COOKIE TIP:

Can't find football-shaped cookies? Frost round cookies with green frosting, use white frosting to pipe on yard lines, and add a brown peanut M&M® as a football.

1. Spread the cookies with chocolate frosting.

2. Place the vanilla frosting into a piping bag or zipper-style freezer bag, pressing the frosting down into one of the bottom corners of the bag. If you're using a zipper-style freezer bag, snip off the corner end of the bag, leaving an opening approximately ¼ inch across.

3. Pipe lines of white frosting on the cookie to replicate the look of a football. Repeat with the remaining cookies.

BASKETBALL COOKIES

Makes 12 cookies

1 (16-ounce) can vanilla frosting

Orange food coloring

Brown food coloring

12 medium-to-large round cookies (any kind)

½ cup chocolate frosting

1. Place the vanilla frosting in a microwave-safe bowl and heat for 10 seconds. Remove from the microwave and stir well. If the frosting is a consistency similar to syrup, it is ready to coat the cookies. If it's too thick, return it to the microwave for 5 additional seconds, remove, stir, and repeat until the frosting has a syruplike consistency.

2. Add two drops of orange food coloring and one drop of brown food coloring to the vanilla frosting, and stir well until combined.

3. Place the cookies on a wire rack on top of a baking sheet lined with waxed or parchment paper to catch excess frosting. Either pour or spoon melted frosting over the top of each cookie, completely covering the entire top and sides. Allow the cookies to dry for at least 4 hours.

4. Place the chocolate frosting into a piping bag or zipper-style freezer bag, pressing the frosting down into one of the bottom corners of the bag. If you're using a zipper-style freezer bag, snip off the corner end of the bag, leaving an opening approximately ¼ inch across.

5. Pipe lines of chocolate frosting on the cookie to replicate the look of a basketball. Repeat with the remaining cookies.

BASEBALL COOKIES

Makes 12 cookies

1 (16-ounce) can vanilla Duncan Hines® Creamy Home-Style Frosting

12 medium-to-large round cookies (any kind)

Red edible marker

1. Place the frosting in a microwave-safe bowl and heat for 10 seconds. Remove from the microwave and stir well. If the frosting is a consistency similar to syrup, it is ready to coat the cookies. If it's too thick, return it to the microwave for 5 additional seconds, remove, stir, and repeat until the frosting has a syruplike consistency.

2. Place the cookies on a wire rack on top of a baking sheet lined with waxed or parchment paper to catch excess frosting. Either pour or spoon the melted frosting over each cookie, completely covering the top and sides. Allow the cookies to dry for at least 4 hours.

3. Use a red edible marker to draw red laces onto the cookies to replicate baseballs.

Beautiful Ballerinas

I'VE BEEN A DANCE MOM *almost as long as I've been a mom. From performances to recitals to competitions to those first pointe shoes, there are always occasions to celebrate. These sweet ballet slipper cookies are cute as can be and will definitely be well received by your favorite ballerina. They also make adorable favors, either packaged in clear jars or in clear, food-safe, cellophane bags. These cookies are perfect for recitals or just to celebrate that pretty pirouette.*

Makes 12 cookies

1 (16-ounce) can Duncan Hines® Creamy Home-Style Strawberries 'N Cream Frosting

12 Nutter Butter® cookies

White candy writer

12 pink candy hearts (about ½ inch in size)

1. Place the frosting in a microwave-safe bowl and heat for 10 seconds. Remove from the microwave and stir well. If the frosting is a consistency similar to syrup, it is ready to coat the cookies. If it's too thick, return it to the microwave for 5 additional seconds, remove, stir, and repeat until the frosting has a syruplike consistency.

2. Place the cookies on a wire rack on top of a baking sheet lined with waxed or parchment paper to catch excess frosting. Either pour or spoon the melted frosting over each cookie, covering the entire top and sides of the cookie. Allow the cookies to dry for at least 4 hours.

3. Prepare the candy writer according to package directions. Use the candy writer to draw a white insole area onto each cookie. Immediately place a candy heart at the base of the white area on each cookie. Allow to dry for at least 2 hours.

Star Student

THESE COOKIES ARE NOT ONLY PERFECT *for your star students, but for their wonderful teachers as well! I have so much gratitude for the teachers my daughters have had, and we also have a number of teachers in my family. My brother and two of my sisters-in-law are teachers, so I definitely believe in doing what we can to show our appreciation. These cute cookies are just one fun way to say thank-you for all your favorite teachers do.*

CHALKBOARD COOKIES

Makes 12 cookies

12 Hershey's® milk chocolate bars (about 18 ounces total)

12 graham cracker sheets

12 tablespoons confectioners' sugar

Brown candy writer

24 white sprinkles

SMART COOKIE TIP:

These fun chalkboard cookies, while perfect for school, can be used for almost any occasion. They look great packaged in a clear, food-safe, cellophane bag tied closed with some fun ribbon.

1. Gently trim the chocolate bars so that they are slightly smaller than the graham cracker sheet.

2. Using a toothpick, carve a message into the backside of a chocolate bar.

3. Sprinkle 1 tablespoon confectioners' sugar over the bar, gently rubbing the sugar into the areas where the message has been etched. Wipe off excess sugar with a slightly damp paper towel.

4. Prepare the brown candy writer according to package directions. Squeeze about 1 to 2 teaspoons of candy coating all over one side of the graham cracker. Immediately place the front side of the chocolate bar onto the graham cracker with candy coating.

5. Use the toothpick to place one or two tiny dots of candy coating on the bottom of the chocolate bar. Press two white sprinkles into the candy coating to replicate the look of chalk. Repeat with the remaining ingredients. Allow to dry for at least 2 hours.

SCHOOLBOOK COOKIES

Makes 12 cookies

12 Mother's® English tea cookies

3 red taffy candies

1 (7-ounce) pouch Betty Crocker® Decorating Cookie Icing

12 school-themed sugar decorations

1. Gently twist open the sandwich cookies.

2. On a surface covered with waxed or parchment paper, roll out the taffy candies with a mini rolling pin to approximately ¼ inch in thickness.

3. Use a small knife or cookie cutter to cut out bookmarks, approximately 1 inch long. Use a small triangle or the bottom of a heart-shaped cookie cutter to cut a small triangle shape out of the bottom of the bookmark.

4. Gently press the taffy bookmark into the filling of the open cookie, then return the top half of the cookie to the sandwich cookie. Repeat with the remaining cookies.

5. Prepare the cookie icing according to package directions. Pipe the cookie icing onto the top of a cookie in a rectangular shape. Immediately place a school-themed sugar decoration onto the icing. Repeat with the remaining cookies. Allow to dry for at least 4 hours.

Goody Goody Gumballs

GROWING UP I ALWAYS THOUGHT *gumball machines were the greatest things. There was something so cool about Mom or Dad giving you a coin, then you'd slowly turn that handle, and boom—a gumball would come out!*

Makes 12 cookies

6 ounces red candy coating

12 Walkers shortbread thistle cookies

Red sanding sugar (about ¼ cup)

6 ounces white candy coating

SweetWorks® Pearls™ or other small round candy balls in assorted colors (about ½ cup)

Black candy writer

12 silver dragées

White sprinkles (about 1 tablespoon)

SMART COOKIE TIP:

*Walker shortbread
thistle cookies are the
perfect shape for
making these cute little
gumball machines!*

1. Prepare the red candy coating according to package directions. Dip the nonround side of a cookie into the coating, sprinkle with red sanding sugar, and place onto a waxed paper–lined baking sheet. Repeat with the remaining cookies. Allow the candy coating to dry for at least 30 minutes.

2. Prepare the white candy coating according to package directions. Let the coating cool slightly because a thick consistency works best for this cookie.

3. Working one cookie at a time, place a spoonful of white candy coating onto the round portion of the cookie, and immediately place the Pearls™ or other round candy balls on the white candy coating. Repeat with the remaining cookies.

4. Prepare the black candy writer according to package directions. Squeeze a small amount of black candy coating on the red portion of each cookie to replicate the candy return of a gumball machine.

5. Place one silver dragée and one white sprinkle onto the black candy coating area of each cookie to replicate a coin and coin slot.

Mr. Robot

WHAT KID DOESN'T LOVE ROBOTS? *These robot cookies are just like real robots in that some assembly is required. The robots are made up of many different cookies all placed next to each other, but not attached. This lets you create a nice-sized robot, with individual serving-sized cookies. The cookies listed are the ones I used, but you can get creative with these and use any cookies and decorations you want. The robot expert in our house is our older daughter, Bella. Bella decorated this robot by herself (great job, B!), so feel free to let your kiddos decorate yours as well.*

*Makes 1 robot
(made with 8 cookies)*

½ (16-ounce) can
vanilla frosting

Black food coloring

4 Walkers shortbread
fingers cookies

2 Nabisco® Lorna
Doone® square-
shaped cookies

2 Mother's® English
tea cookies

Assorted candies
of your choice, for
decorating (Bella used
gumdrops, jelly beans,
Chiclet gum pieces,
Airheads Xtremes®
Sweetly Sour Belts, and
other small candies)

2 candy eyeballs

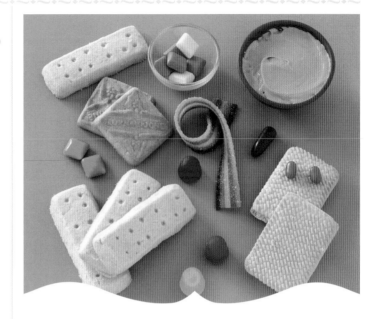

1. Place the frosting in a bowl and add one drop of black food coloring. Mix well to distribute the color. If a darker color is desired, add more food coloring, one drop at a time, stirring well after each addition until the desired shade is achieved.

2. Spread the frosting on the top of each cookie and arrange the cookies into the shape of a robot on a plate or platter that will be used for serving.

3. Stack the two Lorna Doone® cookies on top of each other to give the robot head the same height as the other cookies.

4. Use the assorted candies to create a face and to decorate the arms, legs, and body of the robot. Place the candy eyeballs on the face.

Pretty Princess Wands

HAVING TWO DAUGHTERS, *we've had plenty of princess time in our house. Even if our girls weren't playing princesses, they were always happy to use wands to cast magical spells. These cookie wands are perfect for a fairy princess–themed party. If you can't find star-shaped cookies, use a star-shaped cookie cutter to cut stars out of soft sugar cookies or even graham crackers. If edible glitter isn't available, sanding or crystal sugar will add that touch of sparkle as well.*

Makes 6 cookie wands

12 ounces candy coating in color of your choice

6 medium-to-large star-shaped cookies

6 lollipop sticks or straws

¼ cup edible glitter in color to match your candy coating

1. Prepare the candy coating according to package directions.

2. Lay the star-shaped cookies, backside facing up, on a baking sheet lined with waxed or parchment paper. Allow room for each cookie to have a lollipop stick or straw added.

3. Place a generous spoonful of candy coating onto the center of a cookie, and immediately place a lollipop stick or heavy paper straw into the candy coating. Make sure that the end of the stick or straw is also covered in the candy coating (you can press or twist it into the coating). Repeat with the remaining cookies and place them in the refrigerator for at least 1 hour.

4. If necessary, reheat the candy coating according to package directions. Working one cookie at a time, remove the cookie from the refrigerator and immediately dip or spoon the candy coating onto the star cookie, covering both sides of the cookie. It's important that the end of the lollipop stick or straw be covered in the coating as well, to help make sure it stays firmly attached to the cookie.

5. Sprinkle a small amount of edible glitter over the front of the cookie wand, and place the wand on a baking sheet lined with waxed paper. Repeat with the remaining cookies. Let them set for at least 4 hours.

Smart Cookie

I COULDN'T WRITE A BOOK *called* Smart Cookie *and not include a few smart cookies! These cookies are incredibly easy to make. You start with your favorite bakery-style cookies and use candy writers in colors of your choice to draw on the glasses, lips, noses, and anything you'd like. After drawing on the glasses with the candy writers, place the candy eyes right onto the candy coating and they will set in place. These are fun cookies to make with the kids; they can get pretty creative with the faces they draw!*

Makes 12 cookies

Candy writers in colors of your choice

12 bakery-style cookies

24 large candy eyeballs

1. Prepare the candy writers according to package directions. Use the candy writers to squeeze candy coating on the cookies in the shape of mouths and glasses. Make sure to make the glasses larger than the candy eyeballs.

2. Place the candy eyeballs onto the glasses made from candy coating. Allow to dry for at least 2 hours.

Making Music

MUSIC IS IMPORTANT IN OUR HOUSE. *My husband has played guitar almost his entire life, both my girls love to sing, and my older daughter is working her way through instruments in the school band. We love music! With recitals and performances, there are many chances to celebrate that love of music, and these easy music-note cookies are perfect for that. I used sugar decoration music notes on my cookies, but if you can't find them, you can always pipe some on with chocolate frosting or a black candy writer.*

Makes 12 cookies

1 (7-ounce) pouch white Betty Crocker® Decorating Cookie Icing

12 round cookies, such as sugar or short-bread cookies

2/3 cup chocolate frosting

24 sugar decoration music notes

SMART COOKIE TIP:
You aren't limited to round cookies for these. Feel free to use any shape. Rectangles would be great for replicating sheet music.

1. Prepare the icing according to package directions. Squeeze the icing onto each cookie, covering the top of the cookie. Let dry for at least 4 hours.

2. Place the chocolate frosting in a piping bag or a zipper-style freezer bag, pressing the frosting down into one of the bottom corners of the bag. If you're using a zipper-style freezer bag, snip off the corner end of the bag, leaving an opening approximately 1/4 inch across. Pipe lines of chocolate frosting onto a cookie to replicate lines on sheet music.

3. Place two music-note sugar decorations onto the cookie. Repeat with the remaining cookies.

CHAPTER 7

Cute Creatures

This chapter is full of cookies inspired by cute creatures and critters. These lovely little animals are charming on their own, but many of them will also work wonderfully with children's party themes.

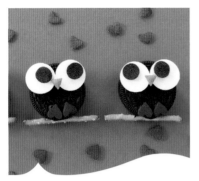

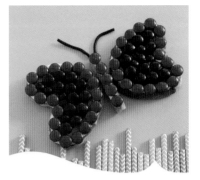

Hoo Wants Cookies?...162

Here Kitty, Kitty...164

Flutter By, Butterfly...166

Good Doggie...168

Little Ladybugs...171

Oh My, Octopi!...173

This Little Piggy...176

Narwhals, Unicorns of the Sea...178

Hoo Wants Cookies?

Everyone loves owls! These owl cookies are quick to throw together and almost too cute to eat. With a few ingredients you can transform Oreo® cookies into these cute little owls. These owls would be great for a fall party, but are also adorable for a woodland creatures party.

Makes 12 cookies

Candy writer in black or white

12 chocolate sandwich cookies

24 round white candy coating discs

24 large black round quins

12 orange candy triangles

24 medium red heart quins

12 small pretzel sticks

1. Prepare the candy writer according to package directions. Working one cookie at a time, assemble the owl. Start by squeezing some candy coating from the candy writer onto the cookie where the eyes will be placed.

2. Gently press two white candy coating discs into the coating to create the eyes. Squeeze a small dot of candy coating onto each white disc, then press a black quin into the candy coating to complete the eyeballs.

3. Squeeze a dab of candy coating onto the white discs where they meet in the middle, and place an orange candy triangle onto the candy coating to create the nose.

4. Squeeze two dabs of candy coating onto the bottom of the cookie, then press two red quin hearts, upside down, onto the cookie to create feet.

5. Squeeze a line of candy coating onto a pretzel stick and press the stick into the opening at the base of the sandwich cookie to create a branch for the owl to perch on. Repeat with the remaining cookies. Let dry for at least 2 hours.

Here Kitty, Kitty

SOME PEOPLE ARE CAT PEOPLE *and some people are not cat people. But almost all people are cookie people, so these fun little felines can enchant everyone! These kitty cats start out as store-bought sugar cookies and are transformed with frosting, sprinkles, and candies. For a fun flavor twist, you can add 1 teaspoon of coconut extract to the vanilla frosting and substitute shredded coconut for the white sprinkles. You will end up with a cookie that looks almost exactly the same, but with coconut flavor. Let the white chocolate candy bars come to room temperature, or warm them slightly in your hands, to make for easy cutting.*

Makes 12 cookies

12 sugar cookies

1 (16-ounce) can white frosting

24 pink candy hearts

12 miniature marshmallows

27 light blue Sweet-Works® Pearls™

2 white chocolate candy bars (about 3½ to 4 ounces each)

White sprinkles (about ½ cup)

White candy writer

Black or brown candy writer

1. Spread the cookies with frosting.

2. Place a pink heart on each cookie for a nose and a pink heart, upside down, on each cookie for a tongue.

3. Use a knife to cut the miniature marshmallows in half, and place two halves on each cookie to create cheeks.

SMART COOKIE TIP:

These kitty cat cookies would also be perfect for Halloween. Simply switch from vanilla frosting and white sprinkles to chocolate frosting and black sprinkles and you have spooky black cats.

4. Place two blue candy Pearls™ on each cookie to create eyes.

5. With a knife, or a triangular cookie cutter, cut small triangles, approximately 1 inch wide, from the candy bar to create ears.

6. Place the candy bar triangles on the cookies to create ears.

7. Garnish the cookies with white sprinkles.

8. Prepare the candy writers according to package directions. Use the white candy writer to draw whiskers onto each cookie, right on top of the sprinkles.

9. Use the black or brown candy writer to make brown dots on the blue Pearls™ to finish off the eyes.

Flutter By, Butterfly

THERE IS ALWAYS SOMETHING A LITTLE MAGICAL *about seeing a butterfly. From visiting our local botanical gardens for their annual butterfly exhibit to raising and releasing our own butterflies, my girls have always enjoyed, and been fascinated by, these delicate creatures. I kept the pieces of these butterfly cookies discrete, making each butterfly out of three separate cookies. I enjoy using multiple cookies to create a dessert—it's almost like an edible puzzle. The cookie shown here is done in the colors of a monarch butterfly, but you can have fun and use any color combination you'd like. Butterflies certainly allow for some creative color choices!*

Makes 6 butterflies

1 (7-ounce) pouch Betty Crocker® Decorating Cookie Icing

12 palmier cookies (also called elephant ear cookies)

1 cup M&M's® chocolate candies

1 cup M&M's® minis chocolate candies

3 Pepperidge Farm® Pirouette® cookies

1 ounce candy coating in color of your choice

Black licorice lace (12 inches long), cut into 1-inch-long segments

1. Prepare the icing according to package directions. Squeeze the icing onto one palmier cookie, covering the entire top surface of the cookie. Immediately decorate with M&M's. Repeat with the remaining palmier cookies.

2. Cut the Pirouette® cookies in half.

3. Apply a line of icing down the center of a Pirouette® cookie and immediately decorate with M&M's. Repeat with the remaining cookies.

4. Place the cookies together to create a butterfly shape.

5. Prepare the candy coating according to package directions. Place a few dabs of the candy coating on the end of two licorice strips and attach to the inside front of the Pirouette® cookie. Repeat with the remaining cookies.

Good Doggie

DOGS HAVE BEEN A PART OF MY FAMILY *my entire life. We have always had at least one canine companion in our home, so I had to make sure they had a place in this book. These cookies are wonderfully cute and a bit over-the-top, with each cookie being made by three cookies! Feel free to mix up your cookies to change the colors to match your favorite pooch. Once you have your base cookie, use one sandwich cookie, divided into two parts, to serve as ears, and one vanilla wafer as part of the face. You can even add frosting to the ears if you want to create the perfect color combo.*

Makes 12 cookies

Black candy writer

12 large chocolate cookies

12 Nutter Butter® cookies, divided into two pieces with filling scraped out

12 vanilla wafers

24 candy eyeballs

12 red SweetWorks® Sixlets®

Black edible marker

1. Prepare the candy writer according to package directions.

2. Use the candy writer to squeeze candy coating on the chocolate cookie where you will place the ears and vanilla wafer face.

3. Place the Nutter Butter® cookies on for ears and the vanilla wafer on for the face.

4. Use the candy writer to squeeze candy coating onto the eye area and place candy eyeballs on top of the coating.

5. Squeeze candy coating onto the back of a Sixlet® and place on the vanilla wafer to create a nose. You may have to hold the Sixlet® in place for a moment until the candy starts to set and holds in place.

6. Use edible marker to draw a mouth onto the vanilla wafer. Repeat with the remaining cookies. Let the candy coating on the cookies dry for at least 2 hours.

Little Ladybugs

I'VE ALWAYS LOVED LADYBUGS. *I remember searching through the grass at recess as a child to find them. I'm not sure if it's the cute name or the pretty red color, but somehow ladybugs just don't seem as buggy as other critters! As a mom, my love of ladybugs continues. Our preschool even has a classroom called The Ladybugs. These ladybug cookies are fun to make and perfect for a garden party.*

Makes 12 cookies

12 ounces red candy coating

12 round sandwich cookies

½ cup mini chocolate chips

6 ounces chocolate or black candy coating

12 small red heart quins

24 white SweetWorks® Pearls™

Black or brown candy writer

1. Prepare the red candy coating according to package directions. Working one cookie at a time, dip the sandwich cookie into the red candy coating, covering approximately three-quarters of the cookie in coating.

SMART COOKIE TIP:

Substitute pink candy coating for red, and you have a whole new look for your ladybugs.

2. Place the cookie onto a baking sheet lined with waxed or parchment paper. Immediately place between six and ten mini chocolate chips onto the coating to create the ladybug's spots. Repeat with the remaining cookies and allow to dry for at least 1 hour.

3. Prepare the chocolate or black candy coating according to package directions. Working one cookie at a time, dip the uncovered portion of the cookie into the candy coating. Place the cookie on waxed paper.

4. Immediately place a red heart quin, upside down, onto the end of the chocolate or black candy coating to create a nose.

5. Press two white Pearls™ into the candy coating as eyes. Repeat with the remaining cookies.

6. Prepare the black or brown candy writer according to package directions and draw pupils onto the pearls to finish the eyeballs. Squeeze a stripe of candy coating down the center of the red area of each cookie to replicate the division of ladybug wings. Allow to dry for at least 2 hours.

Oh My, Octopi!

I'M NOT SURE WHY, BUT I JUST LOVE THE ANIMALS *from the ocean. Maybe it was all the trips to the aquarium growing up or the ocean-themed cartoon show that seems to always be on. Whatever the reason, these little octopus cookies are simply charming. Make these in whatever color you want and if you can't find meringue cookies, feel free to use another style of cookie; puffy round ones would work well.*

Makes 12 cookies

12 meringue cookies

1 (16-ounce) can vanilla Duncan Hines® Creamy Home-Style Frosting

Food coloring in color of your choice

96 candy gummy worms

6 ounces candy coating in color to match the frosting

24 white SweetWorks® Pearls™

Black edible marker

1. Place the meringue cookies onto a wire rack on a baking sheet lined with waxed or parchment paper.

2. Place the frosting in a microwave-safe bowl and heat for 10 seconds. Remove from the microwave and stir well. The frosting should be the consistency of syrup. If the frosting is too thick, return it to the microwave for an additional 5 seconds, remove, and stir. If it's still too thick, repeat the process until the frosting has the desired consistency.

3. Place two drops of food coloring into the frosting and stir well to combine. Add more food coloring if you'd like a darker shade.

4. Spoon or pour melted frosting over each meringue cookie, covering the top and sides. Allow to dry for at least 2 hours.

5. On a baking sheet lined with waxed paper, place the candy gummy worms in groups of eight, with four on each side, to replicate the look of eight octopus legs. Make sure the gummy worms are touching each other at the center.

6. Prepare the candy coating according to package directions. Place approximately 1 tablespoon of coating onto each group of gummy worms, making sure the coating touches each gummy worm. The candy coating will hold the legs together, as well as hold the meringue cookie to the legs.

7. Place a frosted meringue cookie onto each set of eight legs, gently pressing into the candy coating.

8. Dip one white SweetWorks® Pearl™ at a time into the candy coating, taking care not to cover the entire Pearl™, only about one third of it. Immediately place the Pearl™ onto the meringue cookie and hold it in place until the coating begins to set and the Pearl™ remains in place.

9. Repeat with a second Pearl™, then repeat the process with the remaining cookies and Pearls™. Allow the cookies to dry for at least 2 hours.

10. Using the black edible marker, draw a small dot onto each pearl to replicate pupils.

This Little Piggy

I DON'T KNOW WHY, *but there certainly are a lot of little pigs in children's stories. These little pink piggy cookies are sure to thrill the kids, and are perfect desserts for parties with themes that feature pigs. I used Necco® wafers for my piggy noses, but you could also use pink candy-coated wafers and achieve the same look. If you don't want to use strawberry frosting, feel free to just add a few drops of pink food coloring to your vanilla or cream cheese frosting.*

Makes 12 cookies

12 large sugar cookies

1 (16-ounce) can strawberry frosting

8 pink sugar wafer cookies

24 large candy eyeballs

12 pink Necco® wafers

Wilton® Dab-N-Hold™ edible adhesive

24 small round pink quins

1. Spread each cookie with strawberry frosting.

2. Use a knife to cut the pink sugar wafer cookies into a total of twenty-four small triangles to create pig ears.

3. Gently press two pink sugar wafer cookie triangles into the top of each frosted cookie for ears.

4. Place two candy eyeballs onto each cookie.

5. Gently press a pink Necco® wafer into the center of each cookie to create a nose.

6. Place two small drops of Wilton® Dab-N-Hold™ edible adhesive onto each pink Necco® wafer where the nostrils will go.

7. Gently press two round pink quins onto the dots of edible adhesive on each cookie. Allow to dry for at least 20 minutes.

Narwhals, Unicorns of the Sea

AH, THE NARWHAL—UNICORN OF THE SEA! *My daughter Bella and her friend Perri are somewhat obsessed with narwhals. We have narwhal songs, narwhal shirts, and narwhal stuffed animals, so narwhal cookies were a must for this book. These narwhal cookies are for you, B and P! In case the narwhal craze hasn't hit your home, you can always leave the horn off and make these as cute little whale cookies instead.*

Makes 12 cookies

12 Oreo® Double Stuf cookies

Light blue candy writer

12 small blue candy hearts

12 yellow candy tears

1 (16-ounce) can vanilla Duncan Hines® Creamy Home-Style Frosting

Blue food coloring

12 black SweetWorks® Pearls™

12 small blue candy ovals

Black or brown candy writer

1. Place the Oreo® cookies in the freezer for at least one hour.

2. Prepare the light blue candy writer according to package directions. Working one cookie at a time, remove the cookie from the freezer and squeeze a dab of candy coating onto the pointed end of a heart candy.

3. Gently press the candy coating–covered heart end into the side of the cookie, at approximately where the number 3 would appear on a clock. Hold in place until the candy coating sets.

4. Squeeze a generous dab of candy coating onto the large end of a candy tear, then press the candy tear into the side of the cookie, at approximately where the number 11 would appear on a clock. Hold in place until the candy coating sets. Repeat with the remaining cookies.

5. Put the cookies on a wire rack on a baking sheet lined with waxed or parchment paper.

6. Place the frosting in a microwave-safe bowl and heat for 10 seconds. Remove from the microwave and stir well. The frosting should be the consistency of syrup. If the frosting is too thick, return it to the microwave for an additional 5 seconds, remove, and stir. If it is still too thick, repeat the process until the frosting has the desired consistency.

7. Place two drops of blue food coloring into the frosting and stir well to combine. Add more food coloring if a darker shade is desired.

8. Carefully pour or spoon the melted frosting over each cookie. The frosting should cover the heart-shaped tail that was added to the cookie, but should not cover the entire candy tear, only the base.

9. Gently press a black sugar Pearl™ into the frosting on each cookie for an eye, just below the candy tear horn. Press a blue oval candy into the frosting on each cookie as a fin. Allow the cookies to dry for at least 2 hours.

10. Prepare the black or brown candy writer according to package directions. Squeeze a small amount onto each cookie to create a mouth.

Formulas for Metric Conversion

Ounces to grams: *multiply ounces by 28.35*
Pounds to grams: *multiply pounds by 453.5*
Cups to liters: *multiply cups by .24*
Fahrenheit to Centigrade: *subtract 32 from Fahrenheit, multiply by 5 and divide by 9*

Metric Equivalents for Volume

U.S.	METRIC
1/8 tsp.	0.6 ml
1/4 tsp.	1.2 ml
1/2 tsp.	2.5 ml
3/4 tsp.	3.7 ml
1 tsp.	5 ml
11/2 tsp.	7.4 ml
2 tsp.	10 ml
1 Tbsp.	15 ml
11/2 Tbsp.	22 ml
2 Tbsp. *(1/8 cup/1 fl. oz)*	30 ml
3 Tbsp.	45 ml
1/4 cup *(2 fl. oz)*	59 ml
1/3 cup	79 ml
1/2 cup *(4 fl. oz)*	118 ml
2/3 cup	158 ml
3/4 cup *(6 fl. oz)*	178 ml
1 cup *(8 fl. oz)*	237 ml
11/4 cups	300 ml
11/2 cups	355 ml
13/4 cups	425 ml
2 cups *(1 pint/16 fl. oz)*	500 ml
3 cups	725 ml
4 cups *(1 quart/32 fl. oz)*	.95 liters
16 cups *(1 gallon/128 fl. oz)*	3.8 liters

Oven Temperatures

Degrees Fahrenheit	Degrees Centigrade	British Gas Mark
200°	93°	—
250°	120°	1/2
275°	140°	1
300°	150°	2
325°	165°	3
350°	175°	4
375°	190°	5
400°	200°	6
450°	230°	8

Metric Equivalents for Weight

U.S.	METRIC
1 oz	28 g
2 oz	57 g
3 oz	85 g
4 oz	113 g
5 oz	142 g
6 oz	170 g
7 oz	198 g
8 oz	227 g
16 oz (1 lb.)	454 g
2.2 lbs.	1 kilogram

Metric Equivalents for Length

U.S.	METRIC
1/4 inch	.65 cm
1/2 inch	1.25 cm
1 inch	2.50 cm
2 inches	5.00 cm
3 inches	6.00 cm
4 inches	8.00 cm
5 inches	11.00 cm
6 inches	15.00 cm
7 inches	18.00 cm
8 inches	20.00 cm
9 inches	23.00 cm
12 inches	30.50 cm
15 inches	38.00 cm

Resources

ABC Cake Decorating Supplies

Cakearts.com

ABC Cake Decorating Supplies is my favorite supplier for anything baking-related. Located in Phoenix, they have been my go-to supplier for years. They also offer products and assistance online and by phone.

Amazon

Amazon.com

Amazon not only sells packaging supplies, sprinkles, and tools, but they also sell a spectacular variety of cookies as well.

Cakes and Kids

Cakesandkids.com

Cakes And Kids carries a wide variety of sprinkles, party supplies, and packaging supplies.

DK DeleKtables

Etsy.com/shop/dkdelektables

DK DeleKtables carries a wide variety of sprinkles, party supplies, and packaging supplies.

Dylan's Candy Bar

Dylanscandybar.com

Dylan's Candy Bar is a chain of boutique candy shops with the most amazing selection of candy I have ever seen. Any candy you need, Dylan's Candy Bar likely has it.

Fancy Flours

Fancyflours.com

Fancy Flours is a great online resource for baking and decorating. They have great supplies, ideas, and inspiration.

Hobby Lobby
Hobbylobby.com

Hobby Lobby has a great variety of sprinkles and baking products. Make sure to check both the holiday section and baking section of the store if you're looking for seasonal sprinkles.

It's Sugar
Itsugar.com

It's Sugar is a specialty candy store that offers a great variety of hard-to-find candies, many of them in bulk, as well as fun gifts and novelty items. At the time of writing, It's Sugar has stores in more than twenty U.S. states as well as international locations.

Layer Cake Shop
Layercakeshop.com

Layer Cake Shop carries vintage-inspired baking supplies and a great variety of sprinkles.

Michaels
Michaels.com

Most Michaels stores carry a great selection of sprinkles and other baking supplies. They also have a fantastic variety of Wilton® products.

Sweets and Treats Boutique
Shopsweetsandtreats.com

Sweets and Treats Boutique is my favorite supplier for decorative party straws, which I use for my cookie pops. They also have wonderful greaseproof cupcake liners and fun goodie bags.

Wilton
Wilton.com

Wilton is a fabulous resource for everything baking-related, especially decorating supplies.

Acknowledgments

THERE ARE SO MANY PEOPLE who have helped to create *Smart Cookie*.

First and foremost, I want to thank the amazing readers and followers of Love from the Oven. Who knew that sharing my love of sweets and treats would one day result in the book that you are now holding in your hands? I am blessed beyond measure with amazing, creative, inspiring, and kind readers. Thank you, you are the best!

To my incredible agents, Holly Schmidt and Allan Penn, thanks for believing in me, even when I didn't believe in myself. Thank you for taking me on this journey and making me part of the Hollan Family. Your talent, creativity, hard work, and kindness have touched my entire family. You truly are the best. Now can we go listen to Allan sing at Holly Lobby?

To Jordana Tusman, Susan Van Horn, and the team at Running Press, thanks for bringing this book to life!

To Pattie and the team at ABC Cake Decorating Supply, thanks for cheering me on and being the greatest baking supply store a girl could ever ask for.

To my fellow bloggers for always providing support, advice, encouragement, and laughter. What an amazing, inspiring, and wonderful community you all help create each and every day.

To my family, friends, and colleagues, who support me, encourage me, make me laugh, help with my girls, and help make my world go round: Josh and Kim, Grandma Roberta, Jen, Tawnya, Meggan, Alissa, Bobbie, Aunt Joyce, Patti, Kelsi, Erin, Deb, Paige, Risa, Shannon, Katrina, Meghan, Ellie, and Michelle. Sara, thanks for being not only my attorney, but also my friend. Our family is blessed to have your family in our lives.

To my parents, thanks for a lifetime of support, guidance, advice, and love. Mom, thank you for bringing me into the kitchen from a young age, letting me frost, sprinkle, and decorate cookies, starting me down this sweet path, and supporting me all the way. Dad, thanks for always being there for me and for your never-ending supply of encouragement and advice.

To Rick, my husband. This book, my blog, our life—none of it would be without you. You work tirelessly to make life a better place for our family. Thank you for being an incredible husband, an amazing dad, and one heck of a great dishwasher. ILYBAWBAFAIAEL.

To Bella and Grace, my beautiful, creative, amazing, and loving daughters. The two of you are truly the sweetest part of my world. I love you both more than words can ever say. Grace, your smile brightens my world. Bella, your enthusiasm for everything is second to none. You are a rock star, B.

In loving memory of my grandparents: Josie, Joyce, Betty, Paul, and Roy, who taught me to work hard, encouraged my creativity, and always believed in me.

Index

A

Adorable Acorns, 48–49

Airheads Xtremes Sweetly Sour Belts, 36–38, 152–153

Along Came a Spider, 92–93

animals

Flutter By, Butterfly, 166–167

Good Doggie, 168–169

Here Kitty, Kitty, 164–165

Hoo Wants Cookies? 162–163

Little Ladybugs, 170–172

Narwhals, Unicorns of the Sea, 178–180

Oh My, Octopi! 173–175

This Little Piggy, 176–177

B

Baseball Cookies, 143

Basketball Cookies, 142

Beautiful Ballerinas, 144–145

Big Reveal Baby Rattles, 135–137

Birthday Balloons, 118–119

brownies, cookie-topped, 32

By the Campfire, 42–44

C

candy, 24

Candy Buttons, 74–75

candy coating, 16–18

candy corn, 94–96

candy decorating pens, 18

candy eggs, 53–54

candy eyeballs, 24, 45–47, 87, 88–89, 92–93, 94–96, 108–110, 152–153, 156–157, 168–169, 176–177

candy gummy worms, 173–175

candy necklace pieces, 132–134

candy writers, 18

celebrations

Big Reveal Baby Rattles, 135–137

Birthday Balloons, 118–119

Congrats, Graduate! 122–124

Engagement Ring Bling, 125–128

Put on Your Party Hat, 120–121

Then Comes the Baby Carriage, 132–134

Wonderful Wedding Cakes, 129–131

See also holidays

Chalkboard Cookies, 146–147

Chiclets gum squares, 105–107, 152–153

chocolate, 16

chocolate chip cookies

We All Scream for Ice Cream Cones, 63–65

chocolate chips, mini, 90–91, 170–172

chocolate cookies
    Good Doggie, 168–169
    Nice Nests, 53–54
chocolate sandwich cookies
    Along Came a Spider, 92–93
    Congrats, Graduate! 122–124
chow mein noodles, 53–54
Congrats, Graduate! 122–124
Conversation Hearts, 102–104
cookie bark, 32
cookie cutters, 25
cookie parfait, 33
cookie pops, 12, 19
cookie shake, 32
cookies, types of, 11–12
cookie-topped brownies, 32
crumbs, 32–33
crystal sugar, 22
Cupcake Cuties, 76–78

D

dipping, 19, 27–28
disguised cookies
    Candy Buttons, 74–75
    Cupcake Cuties, 76–78
    A Dozen Doughnuts, 66–67
    Faux Cone Snow Cone, 79–81
    Lollipop, Lollipop, 71–73
    Lovely Little Layer Cakes, 60–62
    Mock Macarons, 68–70
    A Slice of Pie, 82–83
    We All Scream for Ice Cream Cones, 63–65

displaying, 31
Down by the Seashore, 55–57
A Dozen Doughnuts, 66–67
dragées, 23

E

Easter Baskets, 111–113
edible glitter, 22
edible markers, 27
elephant ear cookies
    Flutter By, Butterfly, 166–167
Engagement Ring Bling, 125–128
Engagement Ring Cookies, 126–127
equipment, 25
extracts, 13

F

Falling Leaves, 45–47
Faux Cone Snow Cone, 79–81
flavoring, 13, 15
Flutter By, Butterfly, 166–167
food coloring, 13
food coloring pens, 27
Football Cookies, 141
frosting, 13–15, 27, 32, 33. See also icing
Fudge Stripes cookies
    Lucky Leprechaun Hats, 105–107
    Over the Rainbow, 36–38
Fun Flowers, 39–41

G

Ghost Pops, 87

glitter, edible, 22

Good Doggie, 168–169

Goody Goody Gumballs, 149–151

graham crackers
Candy Buttons, 74–75
Chalkboard Cookies, 146–147
Congrats, Graduate! 122–124
Engagement Ring Cookies, 126–127
Faux Cone Snow Cone, 79–81
Save-the-Date Cookies, 128

grocery store bakeries, 11

gumballs, 63–65, 120–121

gumdrops, 152–153

H

Happy Halloween Pops, 86–91

Here Kitty, Kitty, 164–165

Hershey's Kisses, 125–127

holidays
Along Came a Spider, 92–93
Conversation Hearts, 102–104
Easter Baskets, 111–113
Happy Halloween Pops, 86–91
Light the Menorah, 97–99
Little Bunny Pop Pops, 108–110
Lucky Leprechaun Hats, 105–107
O Christmas Tree, 100–101
Sweet Little Turkeys, 94–96
You're a Grand Old Flag, 114–115
See also celebrations

Hoo Wants Cookies? 162–163

I

ice cream cones
Lucky Leprechaun Hats, 105–107
O Christmas Tree, 100–101
We All Scream for Ice Cream Cones, 63–65

icing, 16. See also frosting

J

Jack-O'-Lantern Pops, 90–91

jelly beans, 53–54, 111–113, 152–153

jimmies, 21

Jordan almonds, 97–99, 108–110

K

kids
Beautiful Ballerinas, 144–145
Goody Goody Gumballs, 149–151
Making Music, 158–159
Mr. Robot, 152–153
Play Ball, 140–143
Pretty Princess Wands, 154–155
Smart Cookie, 156–157
Star Student, 146–148

Kraft Jet-Puffed Mallow Bits, 88–89

L

leaf-shaped sandwich cookies
Falling Leaves, 45–47

leftovers, 32–33

licorice laces
black, 90–91, 92–93, 166–167
red, 122–124

Life Savers, 42–44, 132–134
Light the Menorah, 97–99
Little Bunny Pop Pops, 108–110
Little Ladybugs, 170–172
Lollipop, Lollipop, 71–73
lollipops, 39–41, 135–137
Lorna Doone cookies
    Mr. Robot, 152–153
Lovely Little Layer Cakes, 60–62
Lucky Leprechaun Hats, 105–107

M

M&M chocolate candies, 166–167
Making Music, 158–159
markers, edible, 27
Marshmallow PEEPS, 111–113
marshmallows, miniature, 36–38, 42–44,
    108–110, 164–165
melted frosting, 15, 28
Mentos Chewy Mints, 128
meringue cookies
    Oh My, Octopi! 173–175
metric conversions, 181
Mock Macarons, 68–70
Monster Pops, 88–89
Mother's English tea cookies
    Mr. Robot, 152–153
    Schoolbook Cookies, 148
Mr. Robot, 152–153
Murray Sugar Free shortbread cookies
    Engagement Ring Cookies, 126–127
    Fun Flowers, 39–41
    Light the Menorah, 97–99

N

Narwhals, Unicorns of the Sea, 178–180
Necco wafers, 176–177
Nice Nests, 53–54
nonpareils, 22
Nutter Butter cookies, 12
    Adorable Acorns, 48–49
    Beautiful Ballerinas, 144–145
    Good Doggie, 168–169
    Happy Halloween Pops, 86–91
    Sweet Little Turkeys, 94–96

O

O Christmas Tree, 100–101
Oh My, Octopi! 173–175
Oreo cookies, 12
    Hoo Wants Cookies? 162–163
    Light the Menorah, 97–99
    Narwhals, Unicorns of the Sea, 178–180
outdoor themes
    Adorable Acorns, 48–49
    By the Campfire, 42–44
    Down by the Seashore, 55–57
    Falling Leaves, 45–47
    Fun Flowers, 39–41
    Nice Nests, 53–54
    Over the Rainbow, 36–38
    Sweet Snowmen, 50–52
Over the Rainbow, 36–38

P

packaging, 29–30
palmier cookies
 Flutter By, Butterfly, 166–167
paramount crystals, 17
pearls, 23
Pepperidge Farm cookies
 Cupcake Cuties, 76–78
 Pirouette cookies
  Congrats, Graduate! 122–124
  Flutter By, Butterfly, 166–167
  Light the Menorah, 97–99
  You're a Grand Old Flag, 114–115
piping, 27
Play Ball, 140–143
pouring, 28
Pretty Princess Wands, 154–155
pretzel sticks, 42–44, 48–49, 50–52, 162–163
Put on Your Party Hat, 120–121

Q

quins, 22

S

sanding sugar, 22
sandwich cookies, 12
 Big Reveal Baby Rattles, 135–137
 Birthday Balloons, 118–119
 chocolate
  Along Came a Spider, 92–93
  Congrats, Graduate! 122–124
 leaf-shaped
  Falling Leaves, 45–47

Light the Menorah, 97–99
Little Bunny Pop Pops, 108–110
Little Ladybugs, 170–172
Lollipop, Lollipop, 71–73
Save-the-Date Cookies, 128
Schoolbook Cookies, 148
scraps, sweet, 32–33
seasonal cookies, 12
A Slice of Pie, 82–83
Smart Cookie, 156–157
soft cookies, 12
 Lovely Little Layer Cakes, 60–62
 Sweet Snowmen, 50–52
sprinkles, 21–23
Star Student, 146–148
star-shaped cookies
 Pretty Princess Wands, 154–155
sugar
 coloring, 22
 crystal, 22
 sanding, 22
sugar cookies
 By the Campfire, 42–44
 Down by the Seashore, 55–57
 A Dozen Doughnuts, 66–67
 Easter Baskets, 111–113
 Here Kitty, Kitty, 164–165
 Then Comes the Baby Carriage, 132–134
 This Little Piggy, 176–177
 Wonderful Wedding Cakes, 129–131
sugar decorations, 23
sugar wafer cookies, pink
 This Little Piggy, 176–177
sunflower seeds, candy-coated, 94–96

Sweet Little Turkeys, 94–96

sweet scraps, 32–33

Sweet Snowmen, 50–52

T

taffy candies, red, 148

techniques, 27–28

tempering, 16

Then Comes the Baby Carriage, 132–134

thickening, 15

This Little Piggy, 176–177

Tic Tac Freshmints, 50–52

tools, 25

Tootsie Roll Chocholate Midgees, 42–44, 88–89, 90–91

Twizzlers Rainbow Twists licorice, 111–113

V

vanilla wafers

    Down by the Seashore, 55–57

    Good Doggie, 168–169

    Mock Macarons, 68–70

    Then Comes the Baby Carriage, 132–134

W

Walkers shortbread cookies

    fingers

        Mr. Robot, 152–153

    hearts

        Conversation Hearts, 102–104

    thistle

        Goody Goody Gumballs, 149–151

    triangle

        Faux Cone Snow Cone, 79–81

        Put on Your Party Hat, 120–121

        A Slice of Pie, 82–83

We All Scream for Ice Cream Cones, 63–65

Wonderful Wedding Cakes, 129–131

Y

You're a Grand Old Flag, 114–115